WOMEN'S STUDIES

WOMEN IN SPORTS

AMELIA S. HALLOWAY
EDITOR

Nova
Nova Science Publishers, Inc.
New York

LIBRARY OF CONGRESS CATALOGING-IN-PUBLICATION DATA
Women in sports / Editor, Amelia S. Halloway.   p. cm.
Includes index. ISBN 978-1-61728-161-7 (hardcover)
1. Women athletes--Social conditions. 2. Sports injuries. 3. Sports medicine. I. Halloway, Amelia S.
GV709.W574 2010
796.082--dc22
2010016066

Published by Nova Science Publishers, Inc. ✦ New York

183026

£74.50

WOMEN'S STUDIES

WOMEN IN SPORTS

WOMEN'S STUDIES

Additional books in this series can be found on Nova's website under the Series page.

Additional E-books in this series can be found on Nova's website under the E-books tab.

CONTENTS

PREFACE

Although women and young girls have come a long way since the passage of Title IX some thirty four years ago, there is still a lot to do. The framers of the legislation and later on the guidelines understood that mandating equality in opportunity could not happen overnight, and that is the reason why the guidelines and the three-part participation test are crafted the way they are. History has painted a picture of tremendous growth and acceptance of the female athlete, but she still battles the perception that girls and women are inherently less interested in sports than men and that providing women with opportunities cheats men out of resources. This book gathers and presents topical research in the study of women in sports across a broad spectrum.

Chapter 1 – Historically, high performance coaching has been identified as a male domain, with many women dropping out at, or going no further than, participatory or junior levels. Much of the research to date on women coaches has focused on constraints to their activities. Arguably, such an approach fosters a focus on what stands in the way of women coaches rather than how organizations might support them. The purpose of this research was to examine how organizations provide a supportive environment for volunteer high performance coaches. We explored this purpose using an inter-disciplinary approach that examined both the individual and organizational level by analyzing individual psychological needs as well as organizational values. Eight coaches and two coach managers from two Regional Sport Organizations in New Zealand were interviewed using semi-structured interview techniques. The data were manually coded independently by both researchers. Four broad themes emerged: coach development and competence; the coach as a person; the importance of connections between coaches; and the connections with the organization. The themes were examined both intra and inter-organizationally. The values of one organization fostered an environment conducive to the needs satisfaction of the coaches. The environment within the second organization was less effective but reflected its organizational values. The interdisciplinary approach adopted in this study allowed an examination at the individual and organizational level of how an environment may be created in which high performance coaches flourish. As such, this research may offer alternative viewpoints for sport organizations looking to increase numbers of women coaches.

Chapter 2 – Since the self-repair capability of articular cartilage is very limited, the degeneration of cartilage function is inevitable once injured, preventing women in sports from pursuing a faster, higher, and stronger level, and even forcing them to terminate their training. To restore cartilage function, various methods have been applied by physicians. These include medical treatment, physical therapy, microfracture, osteoarticular autograft transfer, and autologous chondrocyte implantation. Though cartilage regeneration by current methods is successful to some extent, the limitations, such as unsatisfactory effectiveness and long-term outcome, are no longer ignored. New methods for cartilage repair are necessary. Cell-based therapy, especially that using stem cells, is drawing increasing attention. There are some promising results from using bone marrow-derived mesenchymal stem cells as the cell source. Meanwhile, other stem cells, such as embryonic stem cell-derived mesenchymal stem cells and induced pluripotent stem cells, are under preliminary study. In this chapter, the cartilage physiology and pathology of women in sports will be discussed. Following current methods for cartilage repair, the strategy and possibility of applying cell-based therapy with an emphasis on stem cells will be addressed, based on basic research as well as clinical trials.

Chapter 3 – Background - Anterior cruciate ligament (ACL) injury rates are four to eight times as high in women as in men. Several studies have been reported to explain the gender difference in ACL injury rates and several intrinsic and extrinsic risk factors underlying gender disparity are believed to exist. Hormonal effects are considered to be one of the etiological factors for female non-contact ACL injuries. The female hormonal cycle is the striking difference between men and women. During the course of the female menstrual cycle, the absolute levels of sex hormones and the ratio of these hormone concentrations change. Because sex hormones are known to affect the properties of ligament tissue, a number of studies have been conducted to evaluate the role of sex hormones in ACL injury. The purpose of this review is to analyze the published literature to determine if the menstrual cycle is associated with women's ACL injury risk and to provide an objective comparison of the published results.

- Study Design
- Review
- Evidence Acquisition
- Studies included associations between the menstrual cycle and women's ACL injuries are reviewed.
- Results

This review of the literature indicates that the menstrual cycle may have a significant effect on women's ACL injury risk. If the menstrual cycle were divided into preovulatory and postovulatory halves of the menstrual cycle, the results of these published reports would be consistent. Almost all studies reported that the high-risk interval of suffering non-contact ACL injury is within the preovulatory phase and no study has yet to identify the high-risk interval in the postovulatory phase.

Clinical Relevance - These findings suggest that female athletes may be more predisposed to ACL injuries during the preovulatory phase of the menstrual cycle. Intervention programs targeted toward this phase of the menstrual cycle may be effective to reduce the incidence of women's ACL injuries.

Chapter 4 – This chapter is based upon the testimony of Marcia D. Greenberger, Co-President, National Women's Law Center, before the Subcommittee on Higher Education, Lifelong Learning, and Competitiveness of the House Committee on Education and Labor on Building on the Success of 35 Years of Title IX.

Chapter 5 – This chapter is based upon the testimony of Jack Mowatt, Commissioner, Maryland-DC Amateur Softball Association, before the Subcommittee on Higher Education, Lifelong Learning, and Competitiveness of the House Committee on Education and Labor on Building on the Success of 35 Years of Title IX.

Chapter 6 – Are you exercising too much? Eating too little? Have your menstrual periods stopped or become irregular? If so, you may be putting yourself at high risk for several serious problems that could affect your health, your ability to remain active, and your risk for injuries. This chapter outlines the risks of overtraining leading to developing osteoporosis, a disease in which bone density is decreased, leaving your bones vulnerable to fracture (breaking).

Chapter 7 – Enacted nearly four decades ago, Title IX of the Education Amendments of 1972 prohibits discrimination on the basis of sex in federally funded education programs or activities. Although the Title IX regulations bar recipients of federal financial assistance from discriminating on the basis of sex in a wide range of educational programs or activities, such as student admissions, scholarships, and access to courses, the statute is perhaps best known for prohibiting sex discrimination in intercollegiate athletics.

Indeed, the provisions regarding athletics have proved to be one of the more controversial aspects of Title IX. At the center of the debate is a three-part test that the Department of Education (ED) uses to determine whether institutions are providing nondiscriminatory athletic participation opportunities for both male and female students. Proponents of the existing regulations point to the dramatic increases in the number of female athletes in elementary and secondary school, college, and beyond as the ultimate indicator of the statute's success in breaking down barriers against women in sports. In contrast, opponents contend that the Title IX regulations unfairly impose quotas on collegiate sports and force universities to cut men's teams in order to remain in compliance. Critics further argue that the decline in certain men's sports, such as wrestling, is a direct result of Title IX's emphasis on proportionality in men's and women's college sports.

In 2002, ED appointed a commission to study Title IX and to recommend whether or not the athletics provisions should be revised. The Commission on Opportunity in Athletics delivered its final report to the Secretary of Education in 2003. In response, ED issued new guidance in 2003 and 2005 that clarified Title IX policy and the use of the three-part test.

This CRS report provides an overview of Title IX in general and the intercollegiate athletics regulations in particular, as well as a summary of the Commission's report and ED's response and a discussion of legal challenges to the regulations and to the three-part test. For related reports, see CRS Report RS22544, *Title IX and Single Sex Education: A Legal Analysis*, by Jody Feder.

In the 111th Congress, several bills related to Title IX have been introduced, including H.R. 2882, H.Res. 95, H.Res. 114, and S.Res. 55.

Chapter 8 – This chapter is based on the statement of Dominique Dawes, President of the Women's Sports Foundation, before the U.S. Senate Committee on Commerce, Science and Transportation.

Chapter 9 – This chapter is based on the testimony of Donna de Varona, U.S. Olympian and Sports Commentator, before the U.S. Senate Committee on Commerce, Science and Transportation on Promotion and Advancement of Women in Sports.

Chapter 10 – This chapter is based on the testimony of Tara Erickson, before the U.S. Senate Committee on Commerce, Science, and Transportation on Promotion and Advancement of Women in Sports.

Chapter 11 – This chapter is based on the statement of Jennie Finch, Olympic Gold Medalist Softball Player, before the U.S. Senate Committee on Commerce, Science and Transportation on Promotion and Advancement of Women in Sports.

Chapter 12 – This chapter is based on the testimony of Christine Grant, former Athletic Director at the University of Iowa and Associate Professor in the Department of Health and Sports Studies, before the U.S. Senate Committee on Commerce, Science and Transportation on Promotion and Advancement of Women in Sports.

Chapter 13 – This chapter is based on the testimony of Lynette Mund, West Fargo, North Dakota, before the U.S. Senate Committee on Commerce, Science and Transportation on Promotion and Advancement of Women in Sports.

Chapter 14 – This chapter is based on the testimony Testimony of Catherine Anne Reddick, before the U.S. Senate Committee on Commerce, Science and Transportation on Promotion and Advancement of Women in Sports.

Chapter 15 – This chapter is based on the statement of Dorothy "Dot" G. Richardson, M.D., Vice-Chair, President's Council on Physical Fitness and Sports, before the U.S. Senate Committee on Commerce, Science and Transportation on Promotion and Advancement of Women in Sports.

Chapter 16 – This chapter is based on the statement of Judith M. Sweet, Senior Vice-President for Championships and Education Services, National Collegiate Athletic Association, before the U.S. Senate Committee on Commerce, Science and Transportation on Promotion and Advancement of Women in Sports.

In: Women in Sports
Editors: Amelia S. Halloway pp. 1-27

ISBN: 978-1-61728-161-7
© 2010 Nova Science Publishers, Inc.

Chapter 1

AN INTER-DISCIPLINARY APPROACH TO EXAMINING ORGANIZATIONAL SUPPORT FOR HIGH PERFORMANCE WOMEN COACHES

Sally Shaw* and Justine B. Allen
School of Physical Education, University of Otago,
PO Box 56, Dunedin 9054, New Zealand

ABSTRACT

Historically, high performance coaching has been identified as a male domain, with many women dropping out at, or going no further than, participatory or junior levels. Much of the research to date on women coaches has focused on constraints to their activities. Arguably, such an approach fosters a focus on what stands in the way of women coaches rather than how organizations might support them. The purpose of this research was to examine how organizations provide a supportive environment for volunteer high performance coaches. We explored this purpose using an inter-disciplinary approach that examined both the individual and organizational level by analyzing individual psychological needs as well as organizational values. Eight coaches and two coach

---

* Corresponding author: *sally.shaw@otago.ac.nz*, Fax: 0064 3 479 8309, Phone: 0064 3 479 5037.

managers from two Regional Sport Organizations in New Zealand were interviewed using semi-structured interview techniques. The data were manually coded independently by both researchers. Four broad themes emerged: coach development and competence; the coach as a person; the importance of connections between coaches; and the connections with the organization. The themes were examined both intra and inter-organizationally. The values of one organization fostered an environment conducive to the needs satisfaction of the coaches. The environment within the second organization was less effective but reflected its organizational values. The interdisciplinary approach adopted in this study allowed an examination at the individual and organizational level of how an environment may be created in which high performance coaches flourish. As such, this research may offer alternative viewpoints for sport organizations looking to increase numbers of women coaches.

The status of women as high performance coaches has come under increasing scrutiny over the past 30 years. During that time, Acosta and Carpenter (2008) have described increases in funding and participation in women's sport within the post-Title IX American college system, while indicating the simultaneous decline in numbers of women in senior coaching positions within that system. Powerful assumptions regarding women's suitability for grass roots and junior coaching rather than high performance roles have also been examined (Shaw & Hoeber, 2003). The sheer commitment and determination of women coaches to deal with work/family balance within a work environment that demands high hours, long distance travel, and constant reassurance of young athletes, has also been analyzed (Bruening & Dixon, 2007; Dixon & Bruening, 2007).

The international under-representation of women in higher level coaching roles is also reflected in New Zealand, where the present study was conducted, and is clearly illustrated in some recent data from New Zealand's Olympic and Commonwealth Games teams. At the 2006 Commonwealth Games in Melbourne, New Zealand women were under-represented in coaching roles relative to the number of women athletes. Of the 48 coaches, from 18 sports, only 14 (30%) were women compared with almost half of the 249 athletes (NZ Olympic Committee, 2006). Furthermore, at the 2008 Olympics in Beijing, China only 3 (7%) of the 43 coaches were women compared with 46.7% of the competing athletes (NZ Olympic Committee, 2008). These figures are comparable with those documented in the United Kingdom where women accounted for only 10% of Great Britain coaches at the 2004 Olympics compared with 39% of athletes (Women's Sport Foundation, 2007) and in

2000 in Canada where only 11% of national teams were coached by women (Marshall, 2001).

Much of the related research about female coaches has either examined large numbers of participants, e.g. Acosta and Carpenter, or the participants are spread over large numbers of organizations, geographical areas, or sports (Bruening & Dixon, 2007; Dixon & Bruening, 2007). These inquiries have provided large scale and, in the case of Bruening and Dixon's multiple studies, in-depth analyses across different organizations. Studies have also tended to focus on the difficulties faced by women, which are many, in comparison to men (Shaw & Hoeber, 2003), or on women's perceived lack of confidence (e.g. Massey University, 2008). The above research has provided invaluable insight into the experiences of women coaches.

However, there remains a twofold gap within the literature. Firstly, there is a need to introduce coaching managers' ideas into the discussions surrounding women coaches' experiences. As the people who manage coaches, coaching managers have a role to play in their development. While Shaw and Hoeber (2003) focused on managers, they did not provide a full analysis of how coaching managers' own intentions meet with coaches' expectations (Knoppers & Anthonissen, 2008). Equally, while Bruening and Dixon's multiple studies have provided in-depth data on coaches' perspectives on administrators' roles, the managers in those studies are silent. By including coach managers' intentions, researchers may be able to gain insight into how organizational environments are constructed with regards to high performance coaches. Specifically, this will address issues such as organizational structural considerations, for example whether policies or programs are in place to encourage and support women coaches. This approach may also give insight into the creation of organizational culture, for example whether women are valued as high performance coaches by their managers and within their organizations.

We also identify a second gap in the current research into women in high performance coaching. Coaching research has largely neglected the idea of examining coaches as individuals with their own needs within the coaching framework. We suggest that there is a need to apply psychological research to the coaching process to understand how organizational context, such as the lack or provision of female mentors, unequal assumptions of competence and balancing work and personal life (Kilty, 2006), influences women coaches' psychological needs.

The purpose of this research is to combine organizational sociological and psychological approaches in an interdisciplinary study in order to investigate the management of high performance women coaches. This analysis of a combination of psychological and organizational experiences will allow us to present a broader picture of the experiences of women who coach at the high performance level. As such, it will offer insights into the psychological and managerial environments created within sport organizations, and allow mangers to consider the possibilities in their own decision making regarding these coaches. To work towards this purpose, we outline a theoretical framework for interdisciplinary study.

THEORETICAL FRAMEWORK

Dixon and Bruening (2005) called for an integrated approach to understanding experiences within sport organizations. They argued that in order to develop understanding of these experiences, it is necessary to examine the individual, structural aspects of sport organizations, along with social values. We adopt this framework as it provides an opportunity to examine both psychological and organizational experiences. In doing so, we recognize that there is overlap and inter-play between the various aspects of Dixon and Bruening's approach. In the interests of clarity, we present the different levels as discrete.

Individual

In order to address the individual aspect of Dixon and Bruening's (2005) framework, we adopt Self Determination Theory (SDT) (Deci & Ryan, 1985; Ryan & Deci, 2002). This approach has proven useful in understanding individuals' social psychological needs. It posits that the satisfaction of psychological needs is a necessary requirement for psychological health and that the social environment can support or thwart satisfaction of these needs. Three psychological needs are central to SDT. These are the need for autonomy, to feel at the origin of one's behavior; the need for competence, to feel effective in one's dealings with the environment; and the need for relatedness, to feel connected with one's social world (Deci & Ryan, 1985; Ryan & Deci, 2002).

The concept of need satisfaction has also proven to be useful in examinations of work organizations' social context. It provides a basis for delineating aspects of the social context that will support self-determined motivation and related positive outcomes. Furthermore, those in leadership positions are a crucial part of the social environment and therefore have an important role to play in supporting or thwarting need satisfaction. Research in the workplace has provided support for the SDT approach to understanding work motivation (see Gagné & Deci, 2005 for a review). Gagné and Deci's review revealed that a work climate characterized by managerial support for employees' autonomy was related to the satisfaction of needs for autonomy, competence, and relatedness. Managerial autonomy support includes acknowledging subordinates' perspectives, offering choice, and encouraging self-initiation. Gagné & Deci (2005) focused on autonomy supportive management in the for-profit sector, and similar findings have been demonstrated with volunteer workers. For example, in two studies, one with college students and one with volunteer workers, Gagné (2003) found that autonomy support was positively related to need satisfaction.

Structural

In their framework, Dixon and Bruening (2005) define structural aspects as the formal attempts to define organizational life. These considerations include policies, programs, and organizational regulations. In terms of women coaches, structures might include women in coaching programs or affirmative action-type policies. SDT can assist in the understanding of organizational structures because it offers the opportunity to examine whether autonomy, competence and relatedness are satisfied, or even recognized, in the development of organizational structures.

It is at the stage of examining this structural level that a broader sociological approach also becomes useful in the understanding of women's experiences as high performance coaches. That is, by examining the processes that go into the development of organizational structures, and employees' or volunteers' interpretations of policies and programs, it is possible to better understand how organizational constraint and opportunity are created (Ely, Foldy & Scully, 2003; Fielding-Lloyd & Meân, 2008). In this research, we adopt a form of discourse analysis as a tool for analyzing organizational structures. For the purposes of this current discussion, discourses influence, and are influenced by, women coaches' and their managers' experiences. While discourses are by definition influential (Foucault, 1980), one discourse does not necessarily have dominance over others. Rather, some values will be privileged over others at certain times but this influence will ebb and flow over time. Discursive meanings are fluid and fragmented (Knoppers & Anthonissen, 2008). Thus, organizational structures will influence, and be influenced by, the experiences of female high performance coaches and their managers at different times.

In this way, we may examine not only how structures are a mirror of organizational realities but also how they are used to knowingly or unknowingly construct the realities of female high performance women coaches' experiences. For example, for some women, affirmative action may present opportunities to have access to higher coaching positions than would otherwise be the case. The policy may have been developed with the organization's best interests at heart, a genuine attempt to encourage as many qualified coaches as possible to be coaching at the highest levels they can. In this case, an affirmative action policy may have positive meanings for the coach in question, her manager, and other coaches in the organization. Conversely, an affirmative action policy may have been developed under duress, the female coach may face envy or ridicule from her peers, and any promotion through the sport's coaching echelons may be perceived as favoritism or reverse sexism (Shaw & Penney, 2003). The influence of a policy that influences organizational structure thus shapes and is shaped by women's experiences.

Values

Finally, Dixon and Bruening (2005) suggest that societal and organizational values need to be examined in light of organizational experiences. Here, discursive analysis is again useful in analyzing the powerful nature of values. Hoeber and Frisby (2001) and Hoeber (2008) have argued that organizational values are fragmented, with different meanings and influence attributed to them. Values are influential, as they encourage employees and volunteers to think and act in certain ways within their organizations. However, they are also fluid, and can be influenced and altered. It is important, therefore, in an analysis of how women coaches are managed, to investigate the values that underpin their management. It is also useful to examine how the coaches themselves define, identify, and support various values within their organizations.

In summary, Dixon and Bruening's (2005) framework offers us an opportunity to explore the potential for an inter-disciplinary approach in examining women coaches' experiences in sport organizations. We have been able to draw on the psychological and sociological literatures and provide coherency through the individual, structural, and values framework. We now turn to our methodology, indicating how the above framework was utilized in our data collection and analysis phases.

METHODOLOGY

In order to achieve the depth of data that we required for this analysis, we adopted qualitative research methods. This approach provided the opportunity for the coaches to discuss their experiences within their organizations, and coaching managers to describe their intentions when managing coaches and their development. Furthermore, given the focus of Dixon and Bruening's (2005) framework, qualitative methods gave us the opportunity to discuss relatively abstract ideas like values in some depth.

The participants were eight women high performance coaches from two Regional Sports Organizations (RSOs) in one region of New Zealand. The coaches ranged in age from 27 to 54 years ($M = 40.1$ years). Their total years of coaching experience ranged from 7 to 17 years ($M = 12.4$ years). All participants had completed at least Level 2 of a national three-level coaching qualification program in their sport. Seven of the coaches had also attended additional coach education opportunities such as conferences, short courses, and seminars. Only one of the eight coaches was employed as a coach, the other seven were volunteer coaches. Five of the volunteer coaches were employed in secondary or tertiary education.

Two organizations were purposively selected because of their differences in numbers and retention of women coaches. One organization represented a popular sport played by both women and men and had small numbers of women coaches (MixOrg). In contrast, the second organization represented a popular sport played predominantly by women and had large numbers of women coaches (WomOrg). Purposive criterion sampling was used to identify potential participants for the study (Patton, 2002). Female high performance coaches who were either coaching or had coached at the regional under 18/19 years, under 21years, or Open level in the last three years were identified via their Regional Sport Organization (RSO) and invited to participate in the study. High performance coaches were chosen because it is when women begin to compete for coaching jobs at representative or professional levels that their numbers dwindle (Acosta & Carpenter, 2008; Shaw & Hoeber, 2003).

Four coaches from each organization were invited to participate in the study, and all eight agreed to participate.

Interviews were conducted at a location of the participants' choice and lasted approximately 60 minutes. In addition, the coach managers from both RSOs were invited to be interviewed and both accepted. In keeping with our university's ethical procedures regarding confidentiality, the organizations were not named and all participants were given a pseudonym.

Interviews were conducted to examine the day-to-day experiences of female high performance coaches through an analysis of their perceptions of the sport organization social context and their relationship with the RSO. Interviews were semi-structured to provide rich, informative description of the coaches' experiences (Burgess, 1982; Fontana & Frey, 2000). In keeping with semi structured interview and qualitative protocol, the interviews were conversational in nature. This process allows rapport to be developed between the interviewer and participant and supports the expression of the participant's point of view (Burgess, 1982). The interview occurs within a framework of topics to be discussed and the specific questions and probes may vary with the flow of the conversation (Burgess, 1982; Fontana & Frey, 2000). As such, the interview questions were designed to encourage the coaches to describe their experiences within their RSO. In order to examine the individual and structural aspects of the coaches' experiences, an interview guide was developed based on SDT concepts, specifically focusing on aspects of the social context that supported coaches' autonomy, competence, and relatedness. Questions included "What kind of involvement does the organization have in your coaching?"; "What development opportunities have been provided by the organization for your coaching?" and "How would you describe your relationship with other coaches?"

Both researchers made brief research notes about the participants' comments, which could be used as a back up to the audio recordings, and also to substantiate the transcripts (Burgess, 1982). In order to gain insight into the values regarding organizational structures and beliefs, the interview guide was supplemented by more general questions. For example, participants were asked 'what does your organization value in its coaches?' 'how are coaches rewarded?' 'do you have the opportunity to provide feedback to the organization and if so, how?'.

The coach managers were asked similar questions. For example, they were asked 'what involvement does the organization have in developing women coaches?', 'are there pathways for coaches?', and 'how are coaches rewarded for their time and efforts?'.

Data analysis was undertaken through a combination of open and axial coding. The tenets of SDT provided a framework for analysis, and the data were analyzed axially for evidence of support for autonomy, competence and relatedness. However, with our broader agenda in mind, the data were also independently coded by the two researchers in an open approach. In this process, the data were analyzed for features that could give us insight into the fluid, discursive nature of organizational values. In keeping with our desire to analyze women coaches' experiences, and managers' intentions, through their articulation of values as fluid, discursive, fragmented constructs, both authors examined the data for commonalities, contrasts and tensions. Comparison was also made between the coaches' and coach managers' comments. The two researchers discussed these findings. The data were initially managed into thirteen themes, which gave insight into a broad overview of the experiences of high performance coaches. However, some values were only mentioned briefly, for example, the organizational value of "using coaching courses to network", which did not express the overall feeling of the coaches. Nor could such an infrequently mentioned value stand up to conceptual analysis. Consequently, the researchers returned to the initial thirteen themes and re-analyzed them, looking to develop more robust analytical categories with a greater richness of data. After this second phase of data analysis, the initial thirteen potential values for analysis in this research were reduced to four. We achieved this reduction by refreshing our perspective, going back to Bruening and Dixon's (2005) framework and reminding ourselves that we wanted to understand the individual, structural, and values aspects of the coaches' experiences, within the boundaries of psychological and sociological approaches.

Using this approach as a guide, we developed the following four themes: coach development and competence; the coach as a person; the importance of connections between coaches; and the connections with the organization.

RESULTS AND DISCUSSION

In this section, we present the results thematically, using the theoretical framework to analyze them in turn. As we worked through our results, we realized that, in order to avoid repetition and to make the most sense out of the data, it was useful to analyze the structural aspects first, which were largely descriptive, and then examine the implications for individual and values based aspects of those structures.

Coach Development Opportunities

The respondents in MixOrg discussed a lack of coach development pathways. Glenys, a long-standing provincial coach stated:

> it's quite limited and I feel the [Organization] should be doing more to up- skill coaches. 'Cause you sort of feel that you get to a level that you're not really developing ... There's nobody really to take you to the next step. There's no interest either in taking coaches to the next step ... they don't really do much for the coaches. As long as they've got somebody in that slot taking a team, they're not really too worried ... nobody ever really came and evaluated me

Reinforcing this position, Fay noted "I always feel like [the experienced coaches] are a bit bored, wanting to talk about themselves, but not wanting to sort of say, "what did work, what system did you use?" Fay also noted that her age and gender worked against her, saying "there is no pathway. No. I might be old, might be female, but I am still developing, and I am prepared to put the work in to develop as a coach".

The coaches were also aware of the bigger picture and the implications if coaches were not up-skilled. As Lara pointed out "I know that MixOrg really values its younger teams, so [they need] to encourage a role model for the younger kids. If they're not doing anything to develop coaches, they can't really expect the younger ones to learn." Glenys outlined the difficulties in attracting good players to the region if good coaches were not available. She said "unless you're up-skilling your coaches you're not really going [anywhere]...word gets around the country, we're not probably attracting [top athletes] for their [sport]. You know, they'll look at going elsewhere because we don't have an [international player] here." Even when coaches had been proactive about development, they were not necessarily encouraged. Jane explained "I put my name down to be assistant to the U-21 because I thought that would be really good experience, but I never heard back. Then this year I wasn't going to coach because of that [experience]." Interestingly Lara, who had been the U-21 coach during the season to which Jane referred, said "I was the Under 21 coach and I didn't have an assistant. I asked if there was anyone that was keen, and they said there wasn't."

Despite these comments, Nick, the Coach Manager of MixOrg was adamant that there was a clear pathway for coaches to up-skill. Consider this conversation between the first author and Nick:

Interviewer: Are there opportunities to work up ...
CM: Yes
I: The coaching ranks?
CM: Most definitely...There is definitely a pathway there. Anyone who wants resources, information, or how to climb the pathway contacts me.

In contrast, the respondents from WomOrg were clear about their pathways through coach development. Raewyn realized the importance of taking opportunities that were presented. She said:

I thought about it and thought well if I'm going to coach at a higher level I need to put myself out there, attend more of these courses. There are heaps and heaps available. That's what I did, I have been to quite a lot and anything that come up I jumped at, you know, went to everything basically.

It was also clear that the coach manager was integral in encouraging coaches to attend sessions. Jackie described how instrumental Anna, the coach manager, had been in developing coaches. Jackie said "she's always been a real encourager. She's always out there trying to get coaches to get their accreditation and everything." Jackie also noted the importance of encouraging youngsters to coach, saying "for a couple of years now and I think we are encouraging a lot of the younger kids to start coaching. High schools are really having to rely on those senior students to become coaches".

One coach, Pat, the most senior at WomOrg, was less glowing in her descriptions of the organizations. She recognized the importance of feedback, saying 'I just think you can't get better if you don't have the feedback". She also valued mentorship, noting, "I've instigated my own mentor, she's fantastic and she'll come to trainings .. she's available to talk at any state so like, I found that really extremely valuable." However, she felt that the organization's input into her development coach had been a bit weak. Pat said "I've had nothing back from the [Organization]... I mean they've been supportive of me, in any face to face contact ... but I question whether they had enough involvement to actually to know if I was doing a good job of coaching..." She also suggested that there could be a better 'grooming' process for high performance coaches, noting "I do question how proactive some of them [WomOrg] were ...there doesn't appear to be a succession plan of coaching... no grooming of people to try and take over." This comment was reiterated by Jackie, who said "No, I wouldn't say I was groomed [laughing]... more like 'we haven't got a coach would you be interested?'".

Anna identified a fairly informal approach to developing coaches as good. She explained that "it's not formalized but take 'Jackie'. We identified her good qualities ... She's coached club level. We had good comments from her senior coach ... and now she's applied to coach [regional] U-19. So if you took an example of a pathway, that's the right thing to do."

Discussion

There were clear differences between the organizational structures regarding coach development opportunities for MixOrg and WomOrg. Despite Nick's belief that there was a clear organizational pathway for coach development in MixOrg, the coaches were not aware of that pathway, or, if they were, felt that they were discouraged from pursuing it, as in Jane's case. There was, therefore, a disjuncture between the expectations of the coaches and the manager in developing a clear organizational pathway for coach development. The discursive construct of coach pathways was therefore contested within MixOrg, ensuring a level of tension between the coaches' and manager's perspectives. This finding reflects that of Fielding-Lloyd and Meân (2008) who, in their analysis of gender equity programs in soccer, found that resistant discourses could undermine the potential of such programs. The outcome in MixOrg of this resistant or incompatible approach was one in which the discourses embraced by Nick were not those experienced by the coaches. As such, any attempt to promote the pathways was undermined.

In contrast, WomOrg had both a formal and informal approach to up-skilling coaches, which most of the coaches felt worked well. They were made aware of the opportunities for accreditation by the coach manager. Moreover, the coach manager was aware of the importance of being proactive, finding new coaches and encouraging them to gain mentorship. The only coach who did not feel that the organization did enough was Pat. Her experience was at the National League level and it may be that the Board or Coach Manager did not feel that they had the expertise to advise her. On the whole, therefore, in WomOrg, there were more consistent discourses regarding the nature of coaching pathways. With that, and more aligned expectations between the coach manager and the coaches, it is unsurprising that this organizational structure was stronger within WomOrg. As Foucault (1980) has noted, however, there are always competing or differing discourses at play, and this was demonstrated by Pat's comment. Acknowledging and valuing her position will assist in further strengthening the organization's approach to coach development (Hoeber & Frisby 2001).

An outcome of the coach pathway structure was the coaches' sense of support for competence development. Two critical features of the social context that foster a sense of competence are training opportunities and feedback (Gagné & Deci, 2005; Mageau & Vallerand, 2003). All of the coaches in this study expressed an interest in and desire for training opportunities and feedback. The coaches from both organizations felt that their organizations could do more to foster their competence. They felt that this could be achieved through clear development pathways and access to courses, informal post-match/training discussions with other coaches, mentoring-type relationships, debriefing sessions and formal evaluations. Coaches in MixOrg felt that none of these opportunities were available to them. As a result they felt there was a lack of training opportunities and feedback and more generally a lack of support for their competence development as high performance coaches. By not supporting coaches' competence the organization is contributing to an environment that is less conducive to the often desired outcomes such as motivation, performance quality, and retention (Allen & Shaw, 2009; Gagné & Deci, 2005). In contrast, coaches in WomOrg had clear coach development pathways and access to a range of courses. They also had networks amongst coaches where they were able to gain feedback. However, only one coach had a mentor which she had organized herself. As a result the coaches in WomOrg felt there were opportunities and support for their competence development but that there was still room for improvement.

Examining coach development as an organizational value gives further insight into why and how these pathways were developed. First, it was clear in MixOrg that Fay felt that being 'old' and 'female' mitigated against her progression. This finding supports other coaching research, in which women have often been overlooked despite similar or higher coaching accreditation to male coaches (Shaw & Hoeber, 2003). Glenys also understood the value of having international players in the region and how that might help coach and athlete development. In order to be successful and *be seen* to be successful, Glenys argued that the region needed to have good enough coaches to attract international players. Both Fay and Glenys recognized, therefore, that coach development was not just about having coaches who are qualified. Rather, the values surrounding 'success' in coaching need to be addressed to examine what assumptions inform 'success' and whether that has an impact on who is considered a successful coach and why. Despite the apparent transparency of Nick's pathways to coach management, there was some aspect of the values surrounding 'coach development' that precluded the women in MixOrg from progressing. It is possible that this preclusion developed because there was a lack of openness within the organization for discussion regarding coach development as an organizational value. As Hoeber (2008) has argued, assuming that meanings regarding an organizational value are shared limits the development of that value. Recognizing and addressing different perspectives on an organizational value may contribute to its development (Hoeber, 2008).

In contrast in WomOrg, the organizational value of coach pathway development embraced a degree of proactivity and flexibility. While a formal route was encouraged through coach accreditation, it was also recognized that informal approaches to highlighting promising coaches were important. The coach development manager recognized that she had a role to identify and nurture coaches, from high school through to the elite level. The organizational value of coach development was thus regarded highly within WomOrg. The coaches perceived and believed this too, which contrasted sharply to the experiences of the coaches in MixOrg. Following Hoeber (2008) the approach taken by WomOrg may well present a seemingly more complex, flexible scenario. Recognizing the 'messiness' of this value and encouraging coaches to contribute to its development ensures that various organizational voices are recognized and rewarded (Hoeber & Frisby, 2001).

Coach as a Person

With this theme, we define 'coach as a person' as recognizing them as being more than 'just' a coach. In MixOrg, there were various comments about the lack of value other than being just someone to fill a coaching position. Consider Fay's comment:

> I wrote a letter to the Board about it. I know I'm as good as these guys. I said I have got my level 2 qualification, I have successfully coached, I have a PhD, I've given talks about coaching. In fact I have everything the same as [the national league coach] apart from the fact he hasn't got his level 2 [qualification]. Perhaps I should have a gender change.

Fay continued the gender theme, describing how women are overlooked for high performance coaching roles. She said "they [the Board, the RDM] think a good man player is better than a good girl player, so in their heads he will be better at explaining skills and tactics and I think they see men as more clever about [the sport]." Lara reiterated this comment with her own perspective on opinions regarding coaches, noting "Nick'll' say they choose the best person for the job. But it's not transparent. They base their definition of 'best person' on their own qualities. And they're all men."

It was not only gender that was considered to be problematic in terms of being valued as more than just a coach. Glenys summed up a popular theme "I guess at the end of the day they are thankful that somebody is putting the work in and taking their team, and they did take us out for dinner, um which was nice, but I just think at the end of the day they're just quite happy for someone to be in that position and it's a position filled." Jane's experiences of a lack of interest by the coach manager once she had agreed to take on her role reiterated this point. She explained:

> once you get your time you know your [practice] bookings, you just go on doing your thing ... you organize how you're getting up to [away venue] for the weekend or you just sort of do everything yourself...making sure the transport's right, the food's right, the accommodation all that side of it... every single thing you were just totally organizing yourself...MixOrg don't sit down one-on-one with the coaches, ok, what can we book for you.

Fay suggested that being overlooked for higher coaching honors was also in part due to the high value that was put on ex-international stars as coaches. "For me there hasn't been a pathway. Possibly because I never was [an international representative], like I had kids at 21. I mean if I was a [well known international player] I'm sure they would have put me through the ranks."

When questioned about the value of female coaches as people, Nick's approach highlighted the need to encourage them to avoid having chaperones for women's teams:

> When there's male coach, like under 18 girls last year, there'd be a female manager, we've gotta make sure all those, all those sorts of issued are, are dealt with, but um, [women coaches] don't seem to be coming forward looking at the secondary schools, ah whether it's an ambition thing, whether they perceive there are barriers ...there's no prejudice towards a female applying for a position at all.

He could also see the value in increasing numbers of women coaches so that he had greater choice regarding coach selection. He noted:

> well two years ago we had way more coaches applying for positions, than actually were positions, we've never had that before. This last year was

a few more and this year I believe there's gonna be a lot more. So then you can hire and fire.

In WomOrg, the coaches' experiences were somewhat different. The strengths and weaknesses of the coaches were recognized and valued. Jackie noted that "they [WomOrg] recognize that the coaches are all individuals and have their own strengths too...if I need any help with anything I would go through the organization." Equally, Raewyn noted that "in terms of our planning and the way the team runs they [WomOrg] don't have any involvement but in terms of organization and going away on trips and all the bits and pieces that goes with that they're really proactive." The organization was even willing to get extra funding for a specialist coaching apprenticeship because they valued the input that Jackie might have. She explained "this coaching apprenticeship is um a [WomOrg] initiative in terms of, they could very well have said 'look we're giving it to Jake' ... but they were happy to seek funding for me as well, they've done great."

Conversations about childcare that highlighted how highly motherhood was valued as a part of the coaches' lives. Raewyn explained:

> The sport is very accommodating with kids, or breastfeeding or whatever has to happen. I like that environment. Jackie's going to a tournament next week, and she was just talking last night about she's taking you know her wee boy with her. And I said look you'll be absolutely fine ... I've done that apprentice coach thing because they are very supportive of that. Some of the courses I've been to there's babies there and it's um it's OK to have your baby there. Whereas I was talking to a friend of mine that when we had our babies we wouldn't have done that, we wouldn't have taken our babies to [sport]; but now it seems to be absolutely fine to do that.

Anna reiterated WomOrg's position by saying "with Jackie, she was breastfeeding and we were happy to make allowances. I haven't heard any negative comments about it."

Discussion

In MixOrg, the coaches were valued just as people who could coach a team, as Glenys argued. This coaching role expanded with the inclusion of the responsibility for booking accommodation and food for tournaments. Structural processes were in place that rewarded them with an annual dinner, which was appreciated. It was, however, quite clear that this was perceived by the coaches as a fairly superficial exercise. To the organization, the coaches were valued in ways that could fulfill structural obligations: to avoid using chaperones and providing choice, thus enabling the organization to 'hire and fire'. There was no mention from Nick of a need to develop a strong base of coaches for the sake of the sport in the region. Kolb, Fletcher, Meyerson, Merrill-Sands, and Ely (2003) have argued that when gender relations are addressed in organizations for purely structural reasons, any short term changes to gender relations are very hard to sustain. This is because structural approaches do not change the culture or informal practices within organizations. Clearly, MixOrg's approach would be unlikely to be sustainable as women with any coaching ambition would likely be deterred by the organizational discourses that did not value them as people, and indeed only value them as chaperones or cannon fodder for hire and fire practices.

In WomOrg, organizational structures were in place which ensured that coaches were valued. Firstly, the removal of responsibility for booking travel and accommodation, and organizing food, ensured that the coaches could focus on coaching and have some time for their other commitments outside coaching. Secondly, the organization's attempts to support women who were mothers, and particularly of very young children, ensured that the organization's structures were in place that valued coaches as women and mothers, not just as coaches. Importantly in WomOrg, following Kolb et al.'s (2003) arguments, there were aspects of the organization that complemented the structural approaches to encouraging the coaches. These aspects, such as a positive approach to coach development discussed above, ensured sustainability within the organization.

A consequence of MixOrg's approach was that coaches had to take sole responsibility for all aspects of their work with athletes. In this respect they were autonomous in their coaching activities. They had choice and opportunities for initiative taking which are features of an autonomy-supportive environment (Gagné & Deci, 2005; Mageau & Vallerand, 2003). However, their autonomy was not supported or fostered. The coaches did not feel that their perspectives were acknowledged, nor that they were recognized and valued as people with different strengths and requirements. In work and education settings managers' and teachers' acknowledgement of subordinates' feelings and perspectives has been shown to be an important feature of an social context that supports psychological needs and desired work behaviors (Deci, Connell, & Ryan, 1989; Deci, Eghrari, Patrick, & Leone, 1994; Gagné & Deci, 2005). Compared with MixOrg, the coaches in WomOrg felt a greater sense of support for their coaching and value as people rather than 'just a coach'. They appreciated the assistance offered by their organization and the recognition that some coaches may need different support such as with childcare. These actions contributed to the coaches feeling that their perspectives were acknowledged, they were valued as people, and consequently that their coaching autonomy was supported.

As an organizational value, the MixOrg coaches recognized two characteristics were vital to being more than 'just a coach': being a man and having an international sporting career. Without these, the coaches did not feel recognized as anything but 'just coaches' who could look after a team. Indeed, despite the coaches going outside the remit of 'coach' by booking accommodation and organizing food and travel, their efforts were arguably not valued by the organization. In MixOrg, it was therefore impossible to argue that the women were valued in any way other than as functional coaches. There were also two key features to this value in WomOrg, which were to remove the stress of booking accommodation from the coaches, and to value them as mothers who were coaches. Motherhood was considered to be part of their coaching persona, rather than a hindrance to it.

Once again, the importance of recognizing and addressing multiple interpretations of an organizational value is highlighted (Hoeber, 2008). To be positively regarded, MixOrg coaches felt they had to have certain characteristics, which they did not possess. They therefore had no association with this organizational value. In WomOrg, the coaches felt that this value was integral to their coaching experience. By examining and analyzing this value, we can better understand it and, hopefully, encourage other organizations to address it.

Connections: Key Organizational Personnel

The coaches in MixOrg had a limited contact with key organizational personnel. As Jane noted, her experience of initiation with the organization had been a case of "here's your balls and cones, so you know, see you later." Fay reiterated this comment with "I mean I don't know if the organization would even care if I wasn't there". It was not just at training sessions that the coaches felt isolated from the organization. Jane described her experience of a weeklong tournament, away from home, with her team:

> when we're away at tournament and stuff we never got one piece of communication from anyone to do with [the province] about how we were

going, like a fax to say good luck with your game or really well done winning this game or yeah. Um, it's important for team spirit as much as anything. It's always nice to, I think if the team, or as a player you feel as though someone's watching out for you and, and seeing how you're getting on.

Interestingly, Nick felt that these representations of support were not accurate. He noted "I do a lot. I've fed them resources, keep in touch all the time and support them as well as I can".

Fay described how she had tried to encourage the organization to invite a famous international coach, who was visiting New Zealand, to the region:

They've got to find money through community trusts or pub charities [NZ funding sources] to keep up-skilling not only their men, you know both male and female. [A top international coach] was in Christchurch with [a national sport organization], get him [to visit] for a weekend, and their answer was, 'oh we'd never get him [to visit]'. I mean that was it, 'no we'd never get him [to visit]. Well why not aim for the top?

In contrast, WomOrg coaches had a relatively open communication with key personnel in the organization. Raewyn noted:

I think just knowing that they are there for you, if you need the help they certainly will help you...[CEO] pops in from time to time ...they're always asking how it's going, is everything OK, is there anything that you need, you know, we want to help you. So no they are there um but you can, I guess you can either choose to use them or work with them or to carry on down and do it yourself.

Pat reiterated the importance of key personnel making coaches feel wanted and useful, saying:

I think making sure people feel valued is huge ...I think just recognizing and thanking people is huge ... Coaches often don't get thanked ...I just think recognizing the time that they give up ... and just support that you're there if you need someone to talk to, but I think definitely a thank you is huge.

Finally, Anna suggested that she was open to even more communication between the coaches and the organization, agreeing that "it's a really good idea to [pursue coach led initiatives]. We should ask them."

Discussion

If structures are in place within sport organizations to ensure that there is good communication between the organization and its coaches, it is likely that the coaches will feel valued and part of the organization. The coaches in MixOrg felt that they were dismissed once they had been selected. This experience, and that of not receiving any encouragement from the organization whilst away on tournament, indicated there were no formal processes by which key organizational personnel kept in touch with their coaches, thus losing important connections with the coaches.

Once again, there are clear contrasts between the organizations in their structural approach to relationships with key personnel. Nick from MixOrg was sure that he was doing all he could to support the coaches by feeding them resources. For the coaches, there was much more to organizational support, including the seemingly small things like contact during a tournament. In contrast, Anna from WomOrg noted the importance of taking account of coaches' perspectives and asking them how the organization could better support them. While the coaches may have felt that there are some missing elements to WomOrg's attempts to develop relationships with key organizational personnel, they certainly recognized and appreciated the structures that were in place. As Scully (2003) and Fine (2003) have noted, it is important that organizational structures enable open communication in order to ensure that members feel that they are a valued part of the organization. Although Nick provided information, he did not enable two way communications, which undermined the women coaches. In contrast, the more open structures in WomOrg ensured that the coaches felt that they were, to some degree, part of the organization.

As a consequence of these structures coaches in MixOrg were far from satisfied with their relationships and communications with key organization personnel. They felt these people had little interest in them, their athletes, or their coaching activities. In contrast, WomOrg coaches had closer connections with the CEO, administrator, and coach manager as a result felt their efforts were recognized and valued. Gagné (2003) described an environment that fosters satisfaction of the psychological needs for autonomy, competence, and relatedness as a context that operates "within a climate of relatedness". The findings from this study indicate that the relationships with key personnel and amongst coaches (see discussion under next theme) are important for satisfaction of coaches' sense of relatedness. Central to the psychological sense of relatedness is a feeling that one is cared for and part of the social context (Deci & Ryan, 2002). Key organization personnel such as coach managers, CEOs, and office administrators provide an important link between the organization and its coaches. Therefore, the relationships between these people are critical to coaches feeling that the organization cares about them and that the coaches are part of the social milieu of their sport.

As an organizational value, connections with key personnel were clearly very important to the coaches. As Dixon and Bruening (2005) note, organizational values are informed by experiences. Those who have a good relationship, mainly in WomOrg, relish that communication and the support it provides. Over time, positive experiences ensure that the value develops to be an important and beneficial one. Pat was clear that this relationship should not be taken for granted and that the continuation of the organization showing gratitude was central to maintaining good relationships. This organizational value should be reinforced and nurtured. Where this had not occurred, largely in MixOrg, the levels of commitment and interest from the coaches were far less evident. As an organizational value, Nick saw the importance of 'arms length' support of giving resources and support but did not seem to be proactive in finding out what else the organization might do for the coaches. Understandably, this could reflect an element of self protection for Nick in a busy environment. However, MixOrg's approach seemed to undermine the enthusiasm and connections that the coaches had with the organization.

Connections between Coaches

This final theme highlighted the importance of understanding the need for coaches to interact frequently with each other for support. Consider the following comments from two of MixOrg's coaches. Fay noted "I've noticed people are quite isolated ... you are so on your own ... I have absolutely nobody to talk to ... the isolation is unbelievable really." Jane backed up her comments by saying:

> you're pretty much, I felt, there on your own ... maybe if they had like, um, like a women mentor, like someone that was really good, and you know working in that role. Cause it kinda is a bit of a men's club down there I guess. It's got that sorta atmosphere about it.

When asked about her experiences away at a tournament and connections with other coaches, Jane provided more information:

no, only really the parents that were there and probably my manager ... she was the manager last year as well, so she, you know quite often commented ... different things that happened the year before that. But no, no one else you know higher about would be aware of anything I wouldn't imagine

The MixOrg coaches also noted that they did not know the other coaches in the organization. Jane described the connection between coaches as "pretty non-existent" and said that "I'd see people at the [sport venue] I wouldn't really know who they were or what team they were coaching, it's pretty terrible really". Lara stated that "I couldn't probably name half of the coaches". The coaches also offered solutions to this isolation, Fay suggesting "I would like to see, probably each of those rep coaches have somebody ... who they can talk to afterwards and have a debrief really...I've noticed people are quite isolated ... you are so on your own...I have absolutely no body to talk to about it." Jane also had ideas regarding improving the situation, noting "I would have loved it ... if I could have gone along to a coaches club, and have an [elite] male and female coach talking about how to select a team or all the things that you actually need to know, and you can take everybody's [ideas] and ...take a bit from everybody."

When questioned about the need for coaches to interact regularly, Nick alluded to an annual 'thank you dinner' for the coaches, saying that it was "crucial, crucial ... vital. The more we can get networking the better ... we now have a lovely thing at a pizza place. There's been speeches and it's a lovely networking occasion". He was unable to provide any examples of ideas to promote more regular contact between the coaches.

In WomOrg, coaches faced the same isolation issues, with Pat noting that "in the end, coaching can be pretty lonely'. The WomOrg coaches managed to establish informal networks to reduce the levels of loneliness. For example, Jane described her experience "you get your kind of networks going like um under 19's and under 21's there [were other coaches] and myself worked reasonably closely together you know ... talk about a game and then we'll go away and have a coffee and talk about ... what we thought about the teams and all that kind of thing." The informality of the process meant that coaches could talk to a number of other coaches, depending on their availability. Raewyn described her connection with Pat and other coaches. She said:

She's not the only one I use ... and I think that's probably really important that that channel is open, that I can go to [Pat] while maybe some stage we might actually be applying for the same position; but still that we can go to each other and talk about things and I think that's really important that we're all in the same [boat] for [the sport] as well, just bettering ourselves.

This informal process was reinforced by Anna, who noted that "yes, people buddy up ... there's a fair amount of competitiveness but at the end of the day we're all striving for the same thing." There was some intent on behalf of the organization to facilitate these connections as, at tournaments, coaches were roomed together if possible. Jackie described the usefulness of this, saying "it was actually nice to have those other coaches that you can shut the door and kick the wall, without it involving the players ... I think that the good part is that when the chips are down they are there for you as well."

Discussion

Neither MixOrg nor WomOrg had a formal structure to enable connections between coaches. However, WomOrg's coaches were clearly more satisfied that they had connections with other coaches that were very supportive. These findings again reinforce the importance of flexibility in developing structural processes or policies within organizations (Kolb et al., 2003).

In part, the coaches' satisfaction may be because the coach manager for WomOrg had an understanding of what the coaches wanted, and was willing to support it, however informally. In contrast, Nick understood coaching connections to mean a one off, end of season networking session run by the organization. While formally sanctioned by MixOrg, and thus considered to be a structural feature of the organization, this networking session did not allow the continual, casual connections between the coaches that were clear in WomOrg. Indeed, it may have been the informal nature of WomOrg's approach that made it successful. This would reinforce Shaw's (2006) findings that informal connections can be very strong within organizations. In WomOrg, the connections between coaches were organized by the coaches, and flexible. Thus, if a situation occurred whereby a coach wanted to discuss coaching with somebody new, they did not have to negate or undermine an existing formal mentorship situation.

As a result of this structure in WomOrg there were well established relationships amongst coaches. These relationships were highly valued, desired by all coaches and contributed to their sense of relatedness. In contrast, the coaches in MixOrg felt little or no connection with other coaches, further limiting their sense of relatedness. As many of the coaches identified that coaching could at times be quite a lonely role and isolating, it is not surprising that all the coaches, regardless of organization, valued or desired connections with other coaches. This desire for connection among coaches is consistent with Kilty's (2006) findings in her research examining challenges to women in coaching. Coaches in both organizations described the potential benefits of these relationships such as receiving feedback, acting as a sounding board, mentoring, or 'just being there' for each other. All of these actions are likely to foster an environment in which coaches support each other and contribute to the satisfaction of the psychological need for relatedness.

As an organizational value, the connections between coaches were perceived quite differently between the two organizations. For the MixOrg coaches, connections were perceived as something of a 'holy grail' that might alleviate the loneliness and frustration of coaching for the organization. Connections were seen as something that needed to be organized by MixOrg for them, in part because the coaches did not know each other and thus did not know where to start. This feature may give another insight into the organization, that is, without common bonds, the coaches looked to the organization to provide them with support, not to each other. As Hoeber and Frisby (2001) noted, however, strong, meaningful organizational values are often those developed by organizational members themselves, rather than handed down by the organization. Had Nick realized this, he could have encouraged the coaches to work more closely with each other. Other than some initial set up effort, this initiative would not impose on his time, if run by the coaches.

In contrast, the WomOrg coaches had taken the initiative to develop and nurture this organizational value. Interestingly, as well as this value being important for them, as coaches, a number noted how in-fighting or protection of knowledge would be detrimental to the game itself. This maturity ensured that while coaches may well be competitive with each other, both for positions and with regard to results, they were all working towards the betterment of the sport. As such, the organizational value of coaching connections went beyond the need for assistance for coaches, which was the feature of MixOrg, and on towards the improvement of the sport as a whole. Again, following Hoeber and Frisby (2001) and Hoeber (2008), it is important to note the multiple discourses that inform this organizational value. It is not a superficial, thin value, rather one that espouses a variety of opinions and standpoints.

CONCLUSION

This research has offered the opportunity to utilize a framework that recognizes the importance of analyzing individual and structural aspects of organizations, as well as values, in attempting to understand an organizational feature, in this case the experiences of women coaches. This framework has allowed us to bring together a psychological and sociological approach to understanding organizational life. Using it, we have noted the similarities and overlap between two approaches that, at first glance, might seem to be quite different.

In addition, this framework has provided the opportunity to examine both managers' and coaches' voices, in the creation and sustaining of the organizational environments. This is unusual in related research, which has tended to focus on the coaches' views (e.g. Shaw & Hoeber, 2003) and has largely neglected managers' views.

This approach has allowed us to describe the structural aspects of organizations but also to examine the consequences at an individual level. Using self-determination theory (Deci & Ryan, 1985; 2002) also helps to explain why these consequences are important to coaches. Furthermore, the examination of values helps to explain why the structural aspects may exist. This analysis then provides possible directions for intervention.

Finally, while our results are not generalizable, we hope that they may provide some ideas for organizations that hope to encourage and support women coaches.

REFERENCES

Acosta, R. V. & Carpenter, L. J. (2008). *Women in intercollegiate sport. A longitudinal study - thirty-one year update.* West Brookfield, MA: The project on women and social change of Smith College and Brooklyn College of the City University of New York.

Allen, J. B. & Shaw, S. (2009). "Everyone rolls up their sleeves and mucks in": Exploring volunteers' motivation and experiences of the motivational climate of a sporting event. *Sport Management Review, 12,* 79-90.

Bruening, J. E. & Dixon, M. A. (2007). Work-family conflict in coaching II: Managing role conflict. *Journal of Sport Management, 21(4),* 471-496.

Burgess, R. G. (Ed.). (1982). *Field research: A sourcebook and field manual.* London: Allen & Unwin.

Deci, E. L., Eghrari, H., Patrick, B. C. & Leone, D. R. (1994). Facilitating internalization: the self-determination theory perspective. *Journal of Personality, 62*, 119-142.

Deci, E. L., Connell, J. P. & Ryan, R. M. (1989). Self-determination in work organization. *Journal of Applied Psychology, 74*, 580-590.

Dixon, M. A. & Bruening, J. E. (2005). Perspectives on work-family conflict in sport. An integrated approach. *Sport Management Review, 8(3)*, 227-255.

Dixon, M. A. & Bruening, J. E. (2007). Work-family conflict in coaching 1: A top down perspective. *Journal of Sport Management, 21(3)*, 377-407.

Ely, R. J., Foldy, E. G. & Scully, M. A. (Eds.). (2003). *Reader in Gender, Work, and Organization*. Malden, MA: Blackwell.

Fielding-Lloyd, B. & Meân, L. J. (2008). Standards and separatism: The discursive construction of gender in English soccer coach education. *Sex Roles, 58*, 24-39.

Fine, M. G. (2003). Building successful multicultural organizations. In R. J. Ely, E. G. Foldy, & M. A. Scully, (Eds.), *Reader in gender, work, and organization*. Malden, MA: Blackwell.

Fontana, A. & Frey, J. H. (2000). From structured questions to negotiated text. In N. K. Denzin, & Y. S. Lincoln, (Eds.), *Handbook of qualitative research* (2 ed., 645-672). Thousand Oaks, CA: Sage.

Foucault, M. (1980). *Power/Knowledge. Selected interviews and other writings*. Toronto: Random House.

Gagné, M. (2003). The role of autonomy support and autonomy orientation in pro-social behavior engagement. *Motivation and Emotion, 27(3)*, 199-223.

Gagné, M. & Deci, E. L. (2005). Self-determination theory and work motivation. *Journal of Organizational Behavior, 26*, 331-362.

Hoeber, L. (2008). Gender equity for athletes: multiple understandings of an organizational value. *Sex Roles, 58*, 58-71.

Hoeber, L. & Frisby, W. (2001). Gender equity for athletes: Rewriting the narrative for this organizational value. *European Sport Management Quarterly, 1*, 179-209.

Kilty, K. (2006). Women in coaching. *The Sport Psychologist, 20*, 222-234.

Knoppers, A. & Anthonissen, A. (2008). Gendered managerial discourses in sport organizations: Multiplicity and complexity. *Sex Roles, 58*, 93-103.

Kolb, D., Fletcher, J. K., Meyerson, D. E., Merrill-Sands, D. & Ely, R. J. (2003). Making change: A framework for promoting gender equity in organizations. In R. J., Ely, E. G. Foldy, & M. A. Scully, (Eds.), *Reader in Gender, Work, and Organization* (10-15). Malden, MA: Blackwell.

Mageau, G. A. & Vallerand, R. J. (2003). The coach-athlete relationship: A motivational model. *Journal of Sports Sciences*, *21*, 883-904.

Massey University. (2008). *Why 'coach' is usally a bloke: research to focus on New Zealand women and sport coaching*. Retrieved 16 September, 2009, from http:// www. massey. ac. nz/ massey/ about-us/ news/ article. cfm? mnarticle=why-coach-is-usually-a-bloke-05-03-2008.

Patton, M. Q. (2002). *Qualitative Evaluation and Research Methods* (2nd ed.). Newberry Park, CA: Sage.

Scully, M. A. (2003). Human resource management: An overview. In R. J., Ely, E. G. Foldy, & M. A. Scully, (Eds.), *Reader in Gender, Work, and Organization* (279-283). Malden MA: Blackwell.

Shaw, S. (2006). Scratching the back of 'Mr X'. Analyzing gendered social processes in sport organizations. *Journal of Sport Management, 20(4)*, 510-534.

Shaw, S. & Hoeber, L. (2003). 'A strong man is direct and a direct woman is a bitch': analyzing discourses of masculinity and femininity and their impact on employment roles in sport organizations. *Journal of Sport Management, 17(4)*, 347-376.

Shaw, S. & Penney, D. (2003). Gender equity policies in National Governing Bodies: An oxymoron or a vehicle for change? *European Sport Management Quarterly, 3*, 78-102

In: Women in Sports   ISBN: 978-1-61728-161-7
Editors: Amelia S. Halloway pp. 29-49   © 2009 Nova Science Publishers, Inc.

Chapter 2

THERAPIES FOR CARTILAGE INJURIES OF WOMEN IN SPORTS: THE WAY TO CITIUS, ALTIUS, AND FORTIUS

*Shufang Zhang[1,2], Yang Zi Jiang[1,2] and Hong Wei Ouyang[1,2] **

[1]Center for Stem Cell and Tissue Engineering, School of Medicine,
Zhejiang University
[2]Division of Sports Medicine, School of Medicine, Zhejiang University

ABSTRACT

Since the self-repair capability of articular cartilage is very limited, the degeneration of cartilage function is inevitable once injured, preventing women in sports from pursuing a faster, higher, and stronger level, and even forcing them to terminate their training. To restore cartilage function, various methods have been applied by physicians. These include medical treatment, physical therapy, microfracture, osteoarticular autograft transfer, and autologous chondrocyte implantation. Though cartilage regeneration by current methods is successful to some extent, the limitations, such as unsatisfactory

---

* Corresponding author: Dr Hong Wei Ouyang, 39 Center for Stem Cell and Tissue Engineering, School of Medicine, Zhejiang, University, 388 Yu Hang Tang Road, Hangzhou, China 310058, Email: hwoy@zju.edu.cn

effectiveness and long-term outcome, are no longer ignored. New methods for cartilage repair are necessary. Cell-based therapy, especially that using stem cells, is drawing increasing attention. There are some promising results from using bone marrow-derived mesenchymal stem cells as the cell source. Meanwhile, other stem cells, such as embryonic stem cell-derived mesenchymal stem cells and induced pluripotent stem cells, are under preliminary study. In this chapter, the cartilage physiology and pathology of women in sports will be discussed. Following current methods for cartilage repair, the strategy and possibility of applying cell-based therapy with an emphasis on stem cells will be addressed, based on basic research as well as clinical trials.

1. INTRODUCTION

Cartilage is a flexible connective tissue with a limited capability for self-repair, without blood vessels, nerve cells, and lymphocytes. It is present in joints, where it functions to reduce friction and provide flexibility. A variety of factors, including heredity, development, metabolism, and mechanical force, may trigger processes of cartilage loss. Females have a smaller cartilage volume, thickness, and surface area, as well as increased cartilage loss with age. Thus females, especially older women, are more vulnerable to cartilage diseases like osteoarthritis (Koay and Athanasiou 2008). Injured cartilage is difficult to regenerate. Women in sports place a high loading demand on cartilage. Particularly, female athletes in running and football exert pressure on their knee joints. Moreover, sports injuries or similar injuries from exercise or training resulting in broken ligaments can lead to instability of the joint and wear on the cartilage over time. This may impede normal performance in female athletes, or even force them to terminate training. Current methods, such as debridement, microfracture, osteoarticular autograft transfer, and chondrocyte implantation, are helpful for cartilage regeneration, yet stem cell-based therapies are under evaluation because of their unlimited self-renewal and chondrogenic differentiation. In this chapter, the cartilage physiology and pathology of women in sports will be discussed. Following current methods for cartilage repair, the strategy and possibility of applying cell-based therapy with an emphasis on stem cells will be addressed, based on basic research as well as clinical trials.

Table 1. Classification and distribution of cartilage

Cartilage	ECM	Distribution
Hyaline cartilage	Collagen type II, proteoglycans (chondroitin sulfate and heparin sulfate)	Most bones of the embryonic skeleton, articular cartilage, epiphyseal plate, costal cartilage, xiphoid cartilage, most laryngeal cartilage, tracheal ring cartilage, nasal septum, cartilage plates in large and medium bronchi.
Elastic cartilage	Elastic fibers (elastin), collagen types I and II, GAG (chondroitin sulfate and heparin sulfate)	Pinna, external auditory canal, Eustachian tube, epiglottis, laryngeal cartilage, cartilage plates in small bronchi.
Fibrocartilage	Collagen type I, GAG (chondroitin sulfate, dermatan sulfate)	Intervertebral disks, pubic symphysis, menisci.

2. PHYSIOLOGY AND PATHOLOGY OF CARTILAGE

2.1. Cartilage Biology

Cartilage derives from the mesenchyme of mesoderm. It is an avascular, aneural, and alymphatic connective tissue. The main components are cells (chondrocytes) and extracellular matrix (ECM). Based on the molecular composition and appearance of the ECM under the light microscope, there are three types of cartilage: hyaline cartilage, elastic cartilage, and fibrocartilage (Table 1) (Kinner, Capito et al. 2005).

Articular cartilage is a specialized form of hyaline cartilage. It transforms the articulating ends of the bones into lubricated, wear-proof, slightly compressible surfaces, which exhibit very little friction (the coefficient of friction is just 1/15th that of ice) (Slomianka 2009). Based on the chondrocyte morphology and arrangement, and the ECM composition and organization, it is divided into four zones: superficial (tangential layer), middle (transitional zone), deep (radial zone), and the zone of calcified cartilage. Generally, cell size, diameter of collagen fibrils, and proteoglycan content increase from the superficial zone to the deep zone (Wang, Rackwitz et al. 2009). In the superficial zone, the chondrocytes are rather small, flattened, and parallel to the surface. The collagen fibrils also lie parallel to the cartilage surface. In the middle zone, the chondrocytes are slightly larger and round. They line up in single or in isogenous group. The collagen fibrils become larger and are orientated obliquely. In the deep zone, large chondrocytes form columns perpendicular to the articulating surface. In the calcified zone, hypertrophic chondrocytes are embedded in the calcified matrix, and connected with the subchondral bone.

There are no blood vessels in cartilage, so articular cartilage is nourished mainly by the synovial fluid. In addition, calcified cartilage can be fed by nutrients from blood vessels that run through it close to the bone. Because of the poor nutrient supply, chondrocytes in the deep parts of thick cartilage may atrophy, eventually die, and the cartilage is gradually converted into bone.

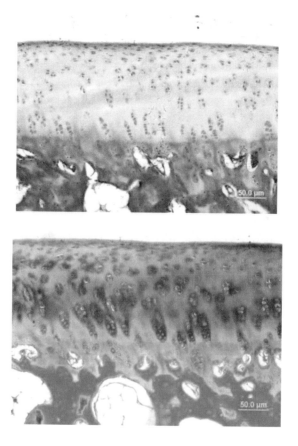

Figure 1. Structure of articular cartilage

Studies to evaluate the physiological differences in cartilage between men and women reveal significant differences in volume, thickness, and surface area. Women have smaller cartilage volume as well as cartilage surface area (Cicuttini, Forbes et al. 1999; Faber, Eckstein et al. 2001; Ding, Cicuttini et al. 2003); the differences are independent of age, body size, and bone size, and increase with age (Cicuttini, Forbes et al. 1999). Besides the volume and surface area, the cartilage thickness in women is also less than in men (Hall and Wyshak 1980; Cova, Frezza et al. 1996). These data demonstrate that gender differences need to be considered when evaluating articular cartilage loss in patients. Regarding the change in knee cartilage volume with age (Ding, Cicuttini et al. 2007), women have substantially greater knee cartilage loss than men, and this gender difference becomes more significant with increasing age over 50. Moreover, the risk for progression of tibiofemoral cartilage defects in women is higher than in men (Cicuttini, Ding et al. 2005; Ding, Garnero et al. 2005; Ding, Cicuttini et al. 2006; Hanna, Teichtahl et al. 2009). These results suggest that both cartilage development and loss in later life contribute to sex differences in cartilage volume.

Regarding the mechanisms for the gender differences in cartilage, many have been proposed, involving differences in physical activity between men and women together with different dynamic forces across the knee joint, hormonal differences (Cicuttini, Forbes et al. 1999), and growth factors (Ding, Cicuttini et al. 2003). The level of high sensitivity C-reactive protein (hsCRP) in serum from women at mid-life makes a significant independent contribution to the variation in the volume of total tibial cartilage (Saxne, Lindell et al. 2003; Hanna, Bell et al. 2008). Exercise participation helps to slow the rate of loss of cartilage volume with age (Wijayaratne, Teichtahl et al. 2008).

2.2. Cartilage Injury

The special nature of the articular cartilage makes it particularly vulnerable. The high demands on the joint surfaces in female athletes and high risk for joint degeneration make treatment of such injuries important to facilitate continued athletic participation and to maintain a physically active lifestyle. There are several ways in which articular cartilage can be damaged:

1. Sudden direct blow to the cartilage (traumatic) e.g. a high-energy injury such as a bad fall directly onto the knee or during sporting

activity. This may happen more often to women who start training without proper instruction.

2. Slow damage to the cartilage following a knee injury (post-traumatic). This may be related to improper treatment or insufficient rest after sport injury.

3. Wear and tear over time (degenerative joint disease) – especially in women athletes who exert repetitive high-weight loading on a certain joint.

4. Immobilization for long periods.

In the general population, articular cartilage damage and osteoarthritis often affect the elderly. However, young people in sports have a high incidence of such problems, either by sudden high loading or wear and tear over time. According to the cartilage injury evaluation system of the International Cartilage Repair Society, articular cartilage defects can be classified into five levels (Table. 2) (Mats Brittberg 2000).

Due to a cartilage defect or damage, many women athletes have to stop training or exercise for a period of time or even for the rest of their life. Loss of function due to trauma or chronic disease may lead to debilitating conditions and osteoarthritis. Osteoarthritis (OA) is a degenerative joint disease, which is characterized by progressive loss of cartilage, increased formation of subchondral bone, and new bone formation at the joint margins (osteophytes). Histological observations have revealed that the normal cartilage structure is totally disrupted in osteoarthritic tissues. The articular surface is fibrillated. Chondrocytes occur in clusters, surrounded by broad acellular areas. Loss of proteoglycan is seen histologically. Females are more susceptible to OA than males at the same age. Women in weight-bearing sports have a 2-3 fold increased risk of radiologic OA of the knees and hips than the general population (Spector, Harris et al. 1996).

In normal healthy women, the baseline tibial plateau area is the main factor affecting the rate of increase of tibial plateau bone area over time (Wang, Wluka et al. 2006). Because of repetitive activity, inadequate rest periods, sudden changes in the type or intensity of training, and sometimes poor or faulty equipment, overuse injuries commonly occur in women athletes. Injuries in the growth plate are general in childhood and adolescence, and can result in apophysitis at multiple sites (Joy, Van Hala et al. 2009). For women athletes who need to increase body weight, obesity has a significant role in tibial bone enlargement and cartilage defects (Wilder and Cicchetti 2009).

Table 2. Grades for cartilage defects, adapted from (Mats Brittberg 2000)

ICRS Grade	Diagram	Defect description
0		Normal and intact articular cartilage
1	A B	Superficial lesions Softening of cartilage surface (A) and/or superficial fissures and cracks of cartilage surface (B)
2		Abnormal Defects occupying <50% of cartilage depth
3	A B C	Severely abnormal Defects occupying >50% of cartilage depth (A), down to calcified zone (B), or down to subchondral bone (C)
4	A B	Severely abnormal Defects penetrating the subchondral lamella (A) or subchondral bone (B)

Studies to decipher the mechanisms underlying cartilage defects or OA in women athletes have been carried out recently. Women athletes have different levels of biomarkers of cartilage degradation. Urinary C-telopeptide of type II collagen (CTx-II) is significantly higher in runners than in non-athlete women (O'Kane, Hutchinson et al. 2006). Generally, knee OA is not genetically related; however, heritability reaches 40% in middle-aged women with bilateral disease from an early age (Felson 2009). A gene that has been confirmed to have an association with OA codes for secreted frizzled-related protein 3 (FRZB). Susceptibility to hip and knee OA in women is associated with functional polymorphisms within FRZB genes (Loughlin, Dowling et al. 2004; Valdes, Loughlin et al. 2007).

3. CURRENT METHODS FOR CARTILAGE REPAIR

Since ulcerated cartilage is not repaired once destroyed, research and clinical trials to understand the mechanism of development and improve therapeutic interventions for cartilage defect repair have been going on for many years. Operative strategies have developed from purely physical methods to combinations of biological and chemical stimulation. Among the cartilage injuries, those to the articular cartilage of the knee are one of the most common causes of permanent disability in athletes (Roos 1998; Drawer and Fuller 2001), so management of this problem is extensively studied. Besides reducing pain, increasing mobility, and improving knee function, the ability to return the athlete to sport and to enable the athlete to continue to perform at the pre-injury level presents one of the most important parameters for a successful outcome from articular cartilage repair in this challenging population.

3.1. Debridement

Debridement is a common treatment for patients whose cartilage defect has not extended to the subchondral bone. This is done by removing the shredded or frayed articular cartilage, fibrous tissue on the meniscus surface, osteophytes, and inflammatory synovial tissue under arthroscopy (Swan, Chapman et al. 1994). This is applicable to grade 1-2 cartilage defects in which the partial thickness of the articular cartilage is damaged (Brittberg and Winalski 2003). After treatment, over 75% of patients are relieved from swelling and pain. However, this treatment is valid for only a very short period (about three months) and it has been combined with other treatments for articular cartilage defect repair.

3.2. Microfracture

Microfracture was first developed by Steadman et al. (Steadman, Rodkey et al. 1999; Steadman, Rodkey et al. 2002). This treatment is based on micropenetration of the subchondral plate and filling the cartilage defect with blood and bone marrow-derived mesenchymal stem cells. This method uses the patient's own healing ability and provides an enriched environment for cartilage regeneration on the chondral surface by thoroughly removing loose fragments and fibrous tissue, and introducing bone marrow-derived mesenchymal stem cells and blood from the bone. It is applicable to grade 3-4 cartilage defects in which the full thickness of the articular cartilage is damaged. After microfracture treatment and following a rehabilitation program, 75-80% of patients experienced significant pain relief and improvement in the ability to perform daily activity and participate in sports, 15% had no change, and 5% continued to deteriorate (LeadingMD 2009).

3.3. Osteoarticular Transfer

Osteoarticular transfer involves harvesting osteoarticular grafts from areas of non-weight bearing articular surfaces in the patient (autograft transfer) or from a tissue bank (allograft transfer), and implanting the grafts into cartilage defects using a press-fit technique. Both autograft and allograft transfers are applicable to grade 3-4 cartilage defects in which the full thickness of the articular cartilage is damaged. Postoperative results demonstrated its efficacy mainly in small or medium-sized full thickness defects (Mithoefer, McAdams et al. 2009), involving decreased pain and improved joint function (Marcacci, Kon et al. 2007). Autograft transfer has been evaluated in athletes over an average of 26 to 36 months (Kish, Modis et al. 1999; Gudas, Kalesinskas et al. 2005). To maintain chondrocyte viability, matrix composition, and the mechanical properties of hypothermically stored cartilage grafts, implantation should be performed within 28 days of graft harvest (Williams, Dreese et al. 2004). There is no study investigating the use of allograft transfer in athletes.

4. CELL-BASED THERAPY FOR CARTILAGE REPAIR

4.1. Chondrocyte Implantation

Allogeneic chondrocyte implantation Isolated allogeneic chondrocyte implantation was first reported by Chesterman and Smith (Chesterman and Smith 1968). This technique is applicable to full-thickness cartilage defects. In animal models, such implantation has been tested to help regeneration of hyaline cartilage and meniscus (Weinand, Peretti et al. 2006). However, pure allogeneic chondrocyte implantation evoked a systemic immunological reaction and the cartilage produced was rejected by the host (Moskalewski, Hyc et al. 2002). As a result, application of this method in clinical trials has been limited.

Autologous chondrocyte implantation (ACI) Brittberg reported the first successful repair of articular cartilage defects in the human knee by ACI (Brittberg, Lindahl et al. 1994). Since approval by the FDA in 1997, it has been performed in more than 20000 patients. It is also applicable to full-thickness cartilage defects. Immune reaction to ACI is prevented by harvesting chondrocytes from an area of the autologous joint that is less weight-bearing, and implanting them into the defective site after *in vitro* multiplication. Successful treatment for hyaline-like restoration of full-thickness articular cartilage defects in the knee has been achieved (Peterson, Minas et al. 2000; Peterson, Brittberg et al. 2002; Knutsen, Engebretsen et al. 2004) and clinical results last for up to 20 years. ACI has also been evaluated in the athletic population (Mithofer, Minas et al. 2005; Mithofer, Peterson et al. 2005). Good to excellent results were demonstrated in 72% to 96%, with improvement of activity scores in 82% to 100%.

The first generation of ACI comprises a two-stage procedure (cell harvest and implantation), which presents adverse effects such as failure, slow tissue maturation, or tissue hypertrophy. Moreover, the phenotype of chondrocytes is unstable when cultured in a 2D environment *in vitro*, and they easily de-differentiate into a fibroblastic cell type, losing the ability to produce cartilage-specific ECM such as collagen type II and aggrecan (Mark 1999). To improve the efficacy of the first generation ACI, second and third generation ACIs have been proposed. Chondrocytes are embedded in collagen gel, fibrin, and alginate, or seeded in a scaffold before implantation (Figure 2). Promising early results have been reported, while the long-term outcome is still under evaluation. Limited cell sources for ACI have led researchers to develop stem cell-based therapies for cartilage defect repair.

4.2. Mesenchymal Stem Cells (MSCs) for Cartilage Repair

MSCs are multipotent stem cells that have the potential to differentiate into many cell types, including chondrocytes, osteoblasts, adipocytes, fibroblasts, stromal cells, muscle cells, and other cells of mesenchymal origin (Tuan, Boland et al. 2003; Giordano, Galderisi et al. 2007; Kolf, Cho et al. 2007). MSCs can be isolated from different tissues, e.g. bone marrow, adipose tissue, synovial membrane, muscle, blood, dermis, and pericytes. Yet bone marrow is considered the most accessible and enriched source of MSCs (Baksh, Song et al. 2004). With proper chemical and mechanical stimulation, MSCs can differentiate into chondrocytes, making them a potent cell source for cartilage defect repair that is receiving considerable attention.

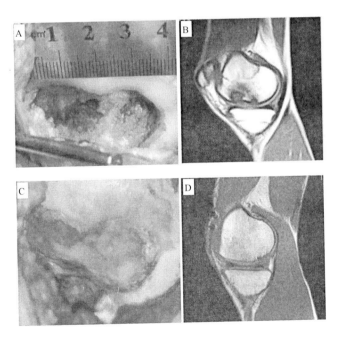

Figure 2. Articular cartilage repair by ACI and evaluation by MRI. Left panels: Intraoperative photographs immediately before (A) and after (C) ACI. Right panels: MRI scans before (B) and 6 months after (D) the procedure

Chondrogenic differentiation of MSCs is carried out in the high-density pellet culture system established by Johnstone and co-workers (Johnstone, Hering et al. 1998). Chemical and mechanical stimulation are combined with this high-density culture system for chondrogenic differentiation of MSCs *in vitro*. Typically, the procedure uses serum-free culture conditions with members of the TGFβ superfamily (TGFβ1, TGFβ3, BMP2, and BMP6) and other bioactive substances which play crucial roles during the induction and progression of chondrogenesis.

Implantation of MSCs *in vivo* demonstrated their potential for chondrogenic differentiation (Ashton, Allen et al. 1980; Goshima, Goldberg et al. 1991). Autologous culture-expanded MSC implantation in a rabbit model showed that articular cartilage defects were repaired (Wakitani, Goto et al. 1994). MSCs were embedded in collagen gel and implanted into large full-thickness cartilage defects. Defect repair was observed as early as 2 weeks after implantation, and subchondral bone was completely repaired by 24 weeks.

MSC implantation was also applied to humans with knee pain. In one clinical trial (Wakitani, Mitsuoka et al. 2004), bone marrow was aspirated from the iliac crest of the patient and MSCs were purified and expanded *in vitro*. Cells were embedded in a collagen gel and implanted into the articular cartilage defect in the patellae. Knee pain was reduced and patients regained their walking ability as soon as 6 months after implantation. The same group carried out another clinical trial in 2007 (Wakitani, Nawata et al. 2007). Three patients with nine full-thickness articular cartilage defects in their knees received transplants of autologous bone marrow-derived MSCs (BMSCs). Improvement of clinical symptoms occurred after 6 months and was maintained for 17-27 months. Complete coverage of the cartilage defects was revealed by MRI. However, fibrocartilaginous tissue, rather than hyaline cartilage, was formed in the defect site. Moreover, BMSCs were used for cartilage defect repair in an athlete. A judo player with a full-thickness cartilage defect had autologous MSCs transplanted into his medial femoral condyle (Kuroda, Ishida et al. 2007). Hyaline-like cartilage tissue was found in the defect site after six months and the patient regained his previous activity level.

4.3. Embryonic Stem Cells (ESCs) for Cartilage Repair

ESCs are pluripotent stem cells derived from the inner cell mass of the blastocyst, are capable of unlimited self-renewal, and differentiate into all derivatives of the three primary germ layers (ectoderm, endoderm, and mesoderm) (Wobus, Holzhausen et al. 1984; Doetschman, Eistetter et al. 1985; Fleming, Haynesworth et al. 1998). Thus, they are considered one of the most promising cell sources for tissue repair.

However, the pluripotency of ESCs makes chondrogenesis challenging for cartilage tissue engineering. Chondrogenic differentiation of ESCs is initiated *in vitro via* cellular aggregates known as embryoid bodies (EBs) (Kramer, Hegert et al. 2000; Kramer, Hegert et al. 2005). This has provided a suitable model to study development *in vitro*. Differentiation in EBs is heterogeneous, resulting in a combination of highly different cell populations. Efforts to improve the chondrogenic differentiation of ESCs via EBs have been made by many research groups. The approaches include screening for an optimal EB size (Messana, Hwang et al. 2008), providing 3D culture environments in scaffolds (Fecek, Yao et al. 2008), co-culture with other cell types such as hepatic cells (Lee, Yu et al. 2008), administering different growth factors such as bone morphogenic proteins (BMPs) and transforming growth factor-β (TGF-β) (Hwang, Kim et al. 2006; Toh, Yang et al. 2007; Yang, Sui et al. 2009), and controlling other environmental factors such as oxygen level (Koay and Athanasiou 2008).

Cartilage repair by implanting ESCs or ESC-derived cells has been under evaluation and positive results have been reported. Repair of osteochondral defects is promoted by implanting ESCs into the defect (Wakitani, Aoki et al. 2004; Dattena, Pilichi et al. 2009). Implantation of ESC-derived chondrogenic cells in mice produces cartilage tissue *in vivo* in 3-4 weeks (Fecek, Yao et al. 2008).

Clinical trials using hESC-derived cells have just passed the first stage. In 2009, the US FDA approved phase I clinical trials of hESC-derived neural stem cell implantation for spinal cord regeneration (Pollack 2009; Reinberg 2009), making possible future studies applying ESCs to the treatment of other severe diseases.

4.4. Induced Pluripotent Stem Cells (iPSCs) for Cartilage Repair

iPSCs are pluripotent stem cells derived from a non-pluripotent cell - an adult somatic cell - by inducing certain genes. iPSCs were first produced from mouse in 2006 (Takahashi and Yamanaka 2006) and from human in 2007 (Takahashi, Tanabe et al. 2007; Yu, Vodyanik et al. 2007). Production of iPSCs was first accomplished by inducing Oct3/4 and Sox3 with either Klf4 and c-Myc or Nanog and Lin28, using retroviruses or lentiviruses to genomically alter the somatic cells. This approach may pose significant risks for humans since the expression of cancer-causing genes or oncogenes may be triggered. The safety concerns have encouraged scientists to explore other production methods. In 2008, mouse iPSCs were produced from fibroblasts without viral vectors (Okita, Nakagawa et al. 2008). Two expression plasmids, one containing the cDNAs of Oct3/4, Sox2, and Klf4, and the other containing the cDNA of c-Myc, were transfected into mouse embryonic fibroblasts and iPSCs were obtained without plasmid integration. Generation of iPSCs without any genetic alteration of the adult cells was demonstrated by the group of Sheng Ding (Zhou, Wu et al. 2009). Mouse fibroblasts were treated with recombinant cell-penetrating reprogramming proteins, and iPSCs produced by this method self-renew over the long-term and are pluripotent both *in vitro* and *in vivo*.

iPSCs have been shown to be identical to natural pluripotent stem cells in many aspects, such as morphology, the expression of certain stem cell genes and proteins, embryoid body formation, teratoma formation, viable chimera formation, and potency and differentiability, allowing researchers to obtain pluripotent stem cells without the problems associated with using embryos. Several groups have reported that iPSCs can differentiate to many cell types, including dendritic cells, macrophages (Senju, Haruta et al. 2009), cardiomyocytes (Tanaka, Tohyama et al. 2009), retinal cells (Hirami, Osakada et al. 2009), adipocytes, and osteoblasts (Tashiro, Inamura et al. 2009). However, the full extent of their relation to natural pluripotent stem cells is still being assessed. Production of iPSCs with high efficiency by suppressing p53 expression (Hong, Takahashi et al. 2009; Krizhanovsky and Lowe 2009) arouses concern over their similarity to cancer cells. The value of iPSCs for therapeutic application needs careful study.

5. CONCLUSIONS

The physiology of cartilage in women differs from that in men in terms of volume, thickness, surface area, and loss with age. Women athletes exert higher loading on their joints, exposing them to higher risk of cartilage injury. Cell-based therapies for cartilage defects or injuries have better therapeutic effects than current methods. Autologous chondrocyte implantation is improved by providing 3D environments for chondrocytes, but its application may be restricted by limited cell sources. Stem cells are considered as potential cell sources because of their unlimited self-renewal and capacity for chondrogenesis. However, the stem cell niche needs to be finely controlled, for committed chondro-lineage differentiation and implantation of embryonic stem cells or induced pluripotent stem cells in humans for cartilage repair still requires support from animal experiments.

REFERENCES

Ashton, B. A. & Allen, T. D. et al. (1980). "Formation of bone and cartilage by marrow stromal cells in diffusion chambers in vivo." *Clin Orthop Relat Res., (151)*, 294-307.

Baksh, D. & Song, L. et al. (2004). "Adult mesenchymal stem cells: characterization, differentiation, and application in cell and gene therapy." *J Cell Mol Med, 8(3)*, 301-16.

Brittberg, M. & Lindahl, A. et al. (1994). "Treatment of deep cartilage defects in the knee with autologous chondrocyte transplantation." *N Engl J Med, 331(14)*, 889-95.

Brittberg, M. & Winalski, C. S. (2003). "Evaluation of cartilage injuries and repair." *J Bone Joint Surg Am, 85-A Suppl 2*, 58-69.

Chesterman, P. J. & Smith, A. U. (1968). "Homotransplantation of articular cartilage and isolated chondrocytes. An experimental study in rabbits." *J Bone Joint Surg, Br, 50(1)*, 184-97.

Cicuttini, F. & Ding, C. et al. (2005). "Association of cartilage defects with loss of knee cartilage in healthy, middle-age adults: a prospective study." *Arthritis Rheum, 52(7)*, 2033-9.

Cicuttini, F. & Forbes, A. et al. (1999). "Gender differences in knee cartilage volume as measured by magnetic resonance imaging." *Osteoarthritis Cartilage, 7(3)*, 265-71.

Cova, M. & Frezza, F. et al. (1996). "[Magnetic resonance assessment of knee joint hyaline cartilage according to age, sex, and body weight]." *Radiol Med, 92(3)*, 171-9.

Dattena, M. & Pilichi, S. et al. (2009). "Sheep embryonic stem-like cells transplanted in full-thickness cartilage defects." *J Tissue Eng Regen Med, 3(3)*, 175-87.

Ding, C. & Cicuttini, F. et al. (2007). "A longitudinal study of the effect of sex and age on rate of change in knee cartilage volume in adults." *Rheumatology (Oxford), 46(2)*, 273-9.

Ding, C. & Cicuttini, F. et al. (2006). "Natural history of knee cartilage defects and factors affecting change." *Arch Intern Med, 166(6)*, 651-8.

Ding, C. & Cicuttini, F. et al. (2003). "Sex differences in knee cartilage volume in adults: role of body and bone size, age and physical activity." *Rheumatology (Oxford), 42(11)*, 1317-23.

Ding, C. & Garnero, P. et al. (2005). "Knee cartilage defects: association with early radiographic osteoarthritis, decreased cartilage volume, increased joint surface area and type II collagen breakdown." *Osteoarthritis Cartilage, 13(3)*, 198-205.

Doetschman, T. C. & Eistetter, H. et al. (1985). "The in vitro development of blastocyst-derived embryonic stem cell lines: formation of visceral yolk sac, blood islands and myocardium." *J Embryol Exp Morphol, 87*, 27-45.

Drawer, S. & Fuller, C. W. (2001). "Propensity for osteoarthritis and lower limb joint pain in retired professional soccer players." *Br J Sports Med, 35(6)*, 402-8.

Faber, S. C. & Eckstein, F. et al. (2001). "Gender differences in knee joint cartilage thickness, volume and articular surface areas: assessment with quantitative three-dimensional MR imaging." *Skeletal Radiol, 30(3)*, 144-50.

Fecek, C. & Yao, D. et al. (2008). "Chondrogenic derivatives of embryonic stem cells seeded into 3D polycaprolactone scaffolds generated cartilage tissue in vivo." *Tissue Eng Part A, 14(8)*, 1403-13.

Felson, D. T. (2009). "Developments in the clinical understanding of osteoarthritis." *Arthritis Res Ther., 11(1)*, 203.

Fleming, J. E., Jr. & Haynesworth, S. E. et al. (1998). "Monoclonal antibody against adult marrow-derived mesenchymal stem cells recognizes developing vasculature in embryonic human skin." *Dev Dyn., 212(1)*, 119-32.

Giordano, A. & Galderisi, U. et al. (2007). "From the laboratory bench to the patient's bedside: an update on clinical trials with mesenchymal stem cells." *J Cell Physiol, 211(1)*, 27-35.

Goshima, J. & Goldberg, V. M. et al. (1991). "The osteogenic potential of culture-expanded rat marrow mesenchymal cells assayed in vivo in calcium phosphate ceramic blocks." *Clin Orthop Relat Res., (262)*, 298-311.

Gudas, R. & Kalesinskas, R. J. et al. (2005). "A prospective randomized clinical study of mosaic osteochondral autologous transplantation versus microfracture for the treatment of osteochondral defects in the knee joint in young athletes." *Arthroscopy, 21(9)*, 1066-75.

Hall, F. M. & Wyshak, G. (1980). "Thickness of articular cartilage in the normal knee." *J Bone Joint Surg Am*, *62(3)*, 408-13.

Hanna, F. S. & Bell, R. J. et al. (2008). "High sensitivity C-reactive protein is associated with lower tibial cartilage volume but not lower patella cartilage volume in healthy women at mid-life." *Arthritis Res Ther.*, *10(1)*, R27.

Hanna, F. S. & Teichtahl, A. J. et al. (2009). "Women have increased rates of cartilage loss and progression of cartilage defects at the knee than men: a gender study of adults without clinical knee osteoarthritis." *Menopause*, *16(4)*, 666-70.

Hirami, Y. & Osakada, F. et al. (2009). "Generation of retinal cells from mouse and human induced pluripotent stem cells." *Neurosci Lett*, *458(3)*, 126-31.

Hong, H. & Takahashi, K. et al. (2009). "Suppression of induced pluripotent stem cell generation by the p53-p21 pathway." *Nature*, *460(7259)*, 1132-5.

Hwang, N. S. & Kim, M. S. et al. (2006). "Effects of three-dimensional culture and growth factors on the chondrogenic differentiation of murine embryonic stem cells." *Stem Cells*, *24(2)*, 284-91.

Johnstone, B. & Hering, T. M. et al. (1998). "In vitro chondrogenesis of bone marrow-derived mesenchymal progenitor cells." *Exp Cell Res.*, *238(1)*, 265-72.

Joy, E. A. & Van Hala, S. et al. (2009). "Health-related concerns of the female athlete: a lifespan approach." *Am Fam Physician*, *79(6)*, 489-95.

Kinner, B. & Capito, R. M. et al. (2005). "Regeneration of articular cartilage." *Adv Biochem Eng Biotechnol*, *94*, 91-123.

Kish, G. & Modis, L. et al. (1999). "Osteochondral mosaicplasty for the treatment of focal chondral and osteochondral lesions of the knee and talus in the athlete. Rationale, indications, techniques, and results." *Clin Sports Med*, *18(1)*, 45-66, vi.

Knutsen, G. & Engebretsen, L. et al. (2004). "Autologous chondrocyte implantation compared with microfracture in the knee. A randomized trial." *J Bone Joint Surg Am*, *86-A(3)*, 455-64.

Koay, E. J. & Athanasiou, K. A. (2008). "Hypoxic chondrogenic differentiation of human embryonic stem cells enhances cartilage protein synthesis and biomechanical functionality." *Osteoarthritis Cartilage*, *16(12)*, 1450-6.

Kolf, C. M. & Cho, E. et al. (2007). "Mesenchymal stromal cells. Biology of adult mesenchymal stem cells: regulation of niche, self-renewal and differentiation." *Arthritis Res Ther.*, *9(1)*, 204.

Kramer, J. & Hegert, C. et al. (2000). "Embryonic stem cell-derived chondrogenic differentiation in vitro: activation by BMP-2 and BMP-4." *Mech Dev, 92(2)*, 193-205.

Kramer, J. & Hegert, C. et al. (2005). "Mouse ES cell lines show a variable degree of chondrogenic differentiation in vitro." *Cell Biol Int., 29(2)*, 139-46.

Krizhanovsky, V. & Lowe, S. W. (2009). "Stem cells: The promises and perils of p53." *Nature, 460(7259)*, 1085-6.

Kuroda, R. & Ishida, K. et al. (2007). "Treatment of a full-thickness articular cartilage defect in the femoral condyle of an athlete with autologous bone-marrow stromal cells." *Osteoarthritis Cartilage, 15(2)*, 226-31.

Leading, MD. (2009). *"microfracture technique."* from http://www.steadman-hawkins.com/knee_microfracture.

Lee, H. J. & Yu, C. et al. (2008). "Enhanced chondrogenic differentiation of embryonic stem cells by coculture with hepatic cells." *Stem Cells Dev, 17(3)*, 555-63.

Loughlin, J. & Dowling, B. et al. (2004). "Functional variants within the secreted frizzled-related protein 3 gene are associated with hip osteoarthritis in females." *Proc Natl Acad Sci U S A, 101(26)*, 9757-62.

Marcacci, M. & Kon, E. et al. (2007). "Arthroscopic autologous osteochondral grafting for cartilage defects of the knee: prospective study results at a minimum 7-year follow-up." *Am J Sports Med, 35(12)*, 2014-21.

Mark, K. v. d. (1999). Structure, biosynthesis and gene regulation of collagens in cartilage and bone. *Dynamics of bone and cartilage metabolism.*

Mats Brittberg, P. A. (2000). Ralph Gambardella, Laszlo Hangody, Hans Jörg Haruselmann, Roland P Jakob, David Levine, Stefan Lohmander, Bert R Mandelbaum, Lars Peterson, Hans-Ulrich Staubli. *"ICRS cartilage injury evaluation package."* from www.cartilage.org.

Messana, J. M. & Hwang, N. S. et al. (2008). "Size of the embryoid body influences chondrogenesis of mouse embryonic stem cells." *J Tissue Eng Regen Med, 2(8)*, 499-506.

Mithoefer, K. & McAdams, T. R. et al. (2009). "Emerging options for treatment of articular cartilage injury in the athlete." *Clin Sports Med, 28(1)*, 25-40.

Mithofer, K. & Minas, T., et al. (2005). "Functional outcome of knee articular cartilage repair in adolescent athletes." *Am J Sports Med, 33(8)*, 1147-53.

Mithofer, K. & Peterson, L. et al. (2005). "Articular cartilage repair in soccer players with autologous chondrocyte transplantation: functional outcome and return to competition." *Am J Sports Med, 33(11)*, 1639-46.

Moskalewski, S. & Hyc, A. et al. (2002). "Immune response by host after allogeneic chondrocyte transplant to the cartilage." *Microsc Res Tech.*, *58(1)*, 3-13.

O'Kane, J. W. & Hutchinson, E. et al. (2006). "Sport-related differences in biomarkers of bone resorption and cartilage degradation in endurance athletes." *Osteoarthritis Cartilage*, *14(1)*, 71-6.

Okita, K. & Nakagawa, M. et al. (2008). "Generation of mouse induced pluripotent stem cells without viral vectors." *Science*, *322(5903)*, 949-53.

Peterson, L. & Brittberg, M. et al. (2002). "Autologous chondrocyte transplantation. Biomechanics and long-term durability." *Am J Sports Med*, *30(1)*, 2-12.

Peterson, L. & Minas, T. et al. (2000). "Two- to 9-year outcome after autologous chondrocyte transplantation of the knee." *Clin Orthop Relat Res*, *(374)*, 212-34.

Pollack, A. (2009). *FDA approves a stem cell trial*. New York.

Reinberg, S. (2009). *FDA OKs 1st Embryonic Stem Cell Trial*. Washington, The Washington Post.

Roos, H. (1998). "Are there long-term sequelae from soccer?" *Clin Sports Med*, *17(4)*, 819-31, viii.

Saxne, T. & Lindell, M. et al. (2003). "Inflammation is a feature of the disease process in early knee joint osteoarthritis." *Rheumatology*, (Oxford) *42(7)*, 903-4.

Senju, S. & Haruta, M. et al. (2009). "Characterization of dendritic cells and macrophages generated by directed differentiation from mouse induced pluripotent stem cells." *Stem Cells*, *27(5)*, 1021-31.

Slomianka, L. (2009, 6th Aug 2009). *"Blue Histology - Skeletal Tissues - Cartilage."* from http:// www. lab. anhb. uwa. edu. au/ mb140/ CorePages/Cartilage/Cartil.htm#CARTILAGE.

Spector, T. D. & Harris, P. A. et al. (1996). "Risk of osteoarthritis associated with long-term weight-bearing sports: a radiologic survey of the hips and knees in female ex-athletes and population controls." *Arthritis Rheum*, *39(6)*, 988-95.

Steadman, J. R. & Rodkey, W. G. et al. (2002). "Microfracture to treat full-thickness chondral defects: surgical technique, rehabilitation, and outcomes." *J Knee Surg.*, *15(3)*, 170-6.

Steadman, J. R. & Rodkey, W. G. et al. (1999). "[The microfracture technic in the management of complete cartilage defects in the knee joint]." *Orthopade*, *28(1)*, 26-32.

Swan, A. & Chapman, B. et al. (1994). "Submicroscopic crystals in osteoarthritic synovial fluids." *Ann Rheum Dis.*, *53(7)*, 467-70.

Takahashi, K. & Tanabe, K. et al. (2007). "Induction of pluripotent stem cells from adult human fibroblasts by defined factors." *Cell*, *131(5)*, 861-72.

Takahashi, K. & Yamanaka, S. (2006). "Induction of pluripotent stem cells from mouse embryonic and adult fibroblast cultures by defined factors." *Cell*, *126(4)*, 663-76.

Tanaka, T. & Tohyama, S. et al. (2009). "In vitro pharmacologic testing using human induced pluripotent stem cell-derived cardiomyocytes." *Biochem Biophys Res Commun.*, *385(4)*, 497-502.

Tashiro, K. & Inamura, M. et al. (2009). "Efficient adipocyte and osteoblast differentiation from mouse induced pluripotent stem cells by adenoviral transduction." *Stem Cells*, *27(8)*, 1802-11.

Toh, W. S. & Yang, Z. et al. (2007). "Effects of culture conditions and bone morphogenetic protein 2 on extent of chondrogenesis from human embryonic stem cells." *Stem Cells*, *25(4)*, 950-60.

Tuan, R. S. & Boland, G. et al. (2003). "Adult mesenchymal stem cells and cell-based tissue engineering." *Arthritis Res Ther.*, *5(1)*, 32-45.

Valdes, A. M. & Loughlin, J. et al. (2007). "Sex and ethnic differences in the association of ASPN, CALM1, COL2A1, COMP, and FRZB with genetic susceptibility to osteoarthritis of the knee." *Arthritis Rheum*, *56(1)*, 137-46.

Wakitani, S. & Aoki, H. et al. (2004). "Embryonic stem cells form articular cartilage, not teratomas, in osteochondral defects of rat joints." *Cell Transplant*, *13(4)*, 331-6.

Wakitani, S. & Goto, T. et al. (1994). "Mesenchymal cell-based repair of large, full-thickness defects of articular cartilage." *J Bone Joint Surg Am*, *76(4)*, 579-92.

Wakitani, S. & Mitsuoka, T. et al. (2004). "Autologous bone marrow stromal cell transplantation for repair of full-thickness articular cartilage defects in human patellae: two case reports." *Cell Transplant*, *13(5)*, 595-600.

Wakitani, S. & Nawata, M. et al. (2007). "Repair of articular cartilage defects in the patello-femoral joint with autologous bone marrow mesenchymal cell transplantation: three case reports involving nine defects in five knees." *J Tissue Eng Regen Med*, *1(1)*, 74-9.

Wang, X. & Rackwitz, L. et al. (2009). " Cartilage development, physiology, pathologies, and regeneration." Strategies in regenerative medicine, Springer New York.

Wang, Y. & Wluka, A. E. et al. (2006). "Factors affecting tibial plateau expansion in healthy women over 2.5 years: a longitudinal study." *Osteoarthritis Cartilage, 14(12)*, 1258-64.

Weinand, C. & Peretti, G. M. et al. (2006). "Healing potential of transplanted allogeneic chondrocytes of three different sources in lesions of the avascular zone of the meniscus: a pilot study." *Arch Orthop Trauma Surg, 126(9)*, 599-605.

Wijayaratne, S. P. & Teichtahl, A. J. et al. (2008). "The determinants of change in patella cartilage volume--a cohort study of healthy middle-aged women." *Rheumatology (Oxford), 47(9)*, 1426-9.

Wilder, R. P. & Cicchetti, M. (2009). "Common injuries in athletes with obesity and diabetes." *Clin Sports Med, 28(3)*, 441-53.

Williams, R. J. & 3rd, Dreese, J. C. et al. (2004). "Chondrocyte survival and material properties of hypothermically stored cartilage: an evaluation of tissue used for osteochondral allograft transplantation." *Am J Sports Med, 32(1)*, 132-9.

Wobus, A. M. & Holzhausen, H. et al. (1984). "Characterization of a pluripotent stem cell line derived from a mouse embryo." *Exp Cell Res., 152(1)*, 212-9.

Yang, Z. & Sui, L. et al. (2009). "Stage-dependent effect of TGF-beta1 on chondrogenic differentiation of human embryonic stem cells." *Stem Cells Dev, 18(6)*, 929-40.

Yu, J. & Vodyanik, M. A. et al. (2007). "Induced pluripotent stem cell lines derived from human somatic cells." *Science, 318(5858)*, 1917-20.

Zhou, H. & Wu, S. et al. (2009). "Generation of induced pluripotent stem cells using recombinant proteins." *Cell Stem Cell, 4(5)*, 381-4.

In: Women in Sports
Editors: Amelia S. Halloway pp. 51-64

ISBN: 978-1-61728-161-7
© 2010 Nova Science Publishers, Inc.

Chapter 3

WOMAN'S ANTERIOR CRUCIATE LIGAMENT INJURIES IN RELATION TO MENSTRUAL CYCLE

Koji Nawata
Department of Sports Medicine and Orthopaedic Surgery,
Sanin Rosai Hospital

ABSTRACT

Background

Anterior cruciate ligament (ACL) injury rates are four to eight times as high in women as in men. Several studies have been reported to explain the gender difference in ACL injury rates and several intrinsic and extrinsic risk factors underlying gender disparity are believed to exist. Hormonal effects are considered to be one of the etiological factors for female non-contact ACL injuries. The female hormonal cycle is the striking difference between men and women. During the course of the female menstrual cycle, the absolute levels of sex hormones and the ratio of these hormone concentrations change. Because sex hormones are known to affect the properties of ligament tissue, a number of studies have been conducted to evaluate the role of sex hormones in ACL injury. The purpose of this review is to analyze the published literature to determine if the menstrual cycle is associated with women's ACL injury risk and to provide an objective comparison of the published results.

Study Design

Review

Evidence Acquisition

Studies included associations between the menstrual cycle and women's ACL injuries are reviewed.

Results

This review of the literature indicates that the menstrual cycle may have a significant effect on women's ACL injury risk. If the menstrual cycle were divided into preovulatory and postovulatory halves of the menstrual cycle, the results of these published reports would be consistent. Almost all studies reported that the high-risk interval of suffering non-contact ACL injury is within the preovulatory phase and no study has yet to identify the high-risk interval in the postovulatory phase.

Clinical Relevance

These findings suggest that female athletes may be more predisposed to ACL injuries during the preovulatory phase of the menstrual cycle. Intervention programs targeted toward this phase of the menstrual cycle may be effective to reduce the incidence of women's ACL injuries.

INTRODUCTION

The incidence of anterior cruciate ligament (ACL) injury remains high in young athletes. In the USA, an estimated 80000 to more than 250000 ACL injuries occur annually many in young athletes 15 to 25 years of age [18]. From the Norwegian data, a total of 2793 primary ACL ligament reconstruction surgeries were registered by 57 hospitals during 18 months.

This corresponds to an annual population incidence of primary ACL reconstruction surgeries of 34 per 100000 citizens (85 per 100000 citizens in the main at-risk age group of 16-39 years) [17]. The majority (70 to 85%) of ACL injuries reported in athletes are non-contact injuries, sustained during sudden deceleration when running, changing direction, or landing from a jump [2].

ACL injury rates are four to eight times as high in women as in men playing at similar levels in the same sports [22,29]. Increased ACL injury risk in teenaged female athletes has increase with the nine fold increase in high school and fivefold increase in collegiate sports in the past 30 years [22]. Several studies have been reported attempting to explain the gender difference in ACL injury rates. Moreover, several intrinsic (those from within the body) and extrinsic (those outside the body) risk factors underlying gender disparity have been proposed [22]. In Hunt Valley, Maryland in 1999, a group of physicians, physical therapists, athletic trainers, and biomechanists interested and engaged in this area of research met to review and summarize data on risk factors for non-contact ACL injury, injury biomechanics, and injury prevention programs. The same group of researchers met again in Atlanta, Georgia in January 2005 to re-evaluate the identified risk factors and to determine what progress had been made since the inaugural meeting in 1999. In these meetings, the risk factors were divided into the following 4 categories: environmental, anatomical, hormonal, and neuromuscular [18].

Hormonal effect is one of these risk factors. The female hormonal cycle is the striking difference between men and women. During the course of the female menstrual cycle, the absolute levels of sex hormones and the ratio of these hormone concentrations change [12,25]. In order to provide a greater understanding of relationship between menstrual cycle phase and non-contact ACL injuries, the objective of this review is to analyze the published literature to determine if non-contact ACL injuries occurred randomly or correlate with a specific phase of the female menstrual cycle in female athletes. It is hypothesized that if these physiological cyclic changes across the menstrual cycle affect the likelihood of the female non-contact ACL injuries, a specific phase for increased incidence of ACL injury might be observed during the menstrual cycle.

The Menstrual Cycle

The menstrual cycle is traditionally divided into two phases (preovulatory and postovulatory phase) or three phases (follicular, ovulatory, and luteal), based on ovarian function. During the course of a normal menstrual cycle, there is a well-defined cascade of hormonal events. The follicular phase, which begins on the first day of menstruation and has a mean length of 9 days, is the most variable in length. During this time, follicles start to develop in the ovary. During the last half of the follicular phase, the diameter of the largest follicle increases rapidly, while the remaining follicles become atretic. Coincident with the development of the largest follicle, the concentration of luteinizing hormon rises. A surge of luteinizing hormone begins 24 hours before ovulation. Associated with this surge is a sharp peak in estrogen output, which occurs before or coincident with the surge in gonadotropins. The ovulatory phase extends over a period of about 5 days. During the last phase, known as the luteal phase (day 15 to the end of the cycle), the follicle collapses and the corpus luteum is formed if pregnancy does not occur. This phase lasts approximately 14 days. A rise in progesterone is seen during the middle of this luteal phase. Consequently, the abrupt cessation of progesterone release determines the onset of menstration. Each phase of the menstrual cycle has a different hormonal environment: low estrogen and low progesterone levels are present during the follicular phase, high estrogen and low progesterone levels are present during the ovulatory phase, and high estrogen and high progesterone levels are present during the luteal phase [9,12,25].

Menstrual Cycle Phase and ACL Injury

Several investigations have studied the relationship between menstrual cycle phase and the risk of woman's non-contact ACL injuries.

In 1998, Wojtys et al [47] were the first to systematically investigate the effects of the menstrual cycle on non-contact ACL injury risk. They used self-reported menstrual history data to characterize the menstrual status of a subject at the time of injury and demonstrated a significantly greater prevalence of non-contact ACL injuries among women athletes during the ovulatory phase of menstrual cycle. In the subsequent study in 2002 [48], the same group measured urine hormone levels to comfirm cycle phase at the time of injury and identified that significantly more ACL injuries occurred during days 9-14 of a 28-day cycle with fewer injuries than expected during the postovulatory phase. In 2007, Adachi et al [1] investigated the relationship of the menstrual cycle phase to non-contact ACL injuries in teenaged female athletes, the high-risk individuals, and also demonstrated a significant increase in non-contact ACL injuries during ovulatory phase.

In 1998, Myklebust et al [32] studied competitive European team handball players across 3 seasons and found an increased risk of non-contact ACL injury during the week before or just after the onset of menstruation. In their subsequent study in 2003 [33], the distribution of non-contact ACL injuries resulted in an increase during the menstrual phase. In 1999, Arendt et al [3] reported an increase in non-contact ACL injuries around menses by the retrospective cohort study which reviewed data submitted to the National Collegiate Athletic Association Injury Surveillance System over 10 years. However, the level of significance was not stated. In 2002, the same authors retrospectively investigated 58 collegiate varsity athletes and reported a significant increase in injuries during the follicular phase and a significant decrease in injuries during the luteal phase [4]. In 2002, Slauterbeck et al [40] used questionnaires and saliva samples within 72 hours of injury to document cycle phase and identified a significantly higher frequency of non-contact ACL injury in days 1 and 2 of the menstrual cycle.

In 2006, Beynnon et al [7] examined the likelihood of suffering an ACL injury by menstrual cycle phase in a case control study of female recreational alpine skiers in the USA. The menstrual cycle was divided into preovulatory and postovulatory phases based on serum progesterone concentrations obtained at the time of injury. They determined that the injury risk was significantly greater during the preovulatory phase of the menstrual cycle compared with the postovulatory phase, with 74% of the injured subjects being in the preovulatory phase, whereas only 56% of the controls were in the preovulatory phase. In 2009, Ruedl et al [35] investigated the female recreational skiers with a non-contact ACL injury and age-matched controls in Austrian Alps. Analysis of menstrual history data revealed that recreational skiers in the preovulatory phase were significantly more likely to sustain an non-contact ACL injury than were skiers in the postovulatory phase. 57% of ACL-injured subjects were in the preovulatory phase, whereas 41% of the controls were in the preovulatory phase at the time of questioning. In these two studies of female alpine skiers, exactly the same distribution was ovserved seen in the data.

At first sight, these findings have been equivocal and there is little consensus in the literature. However, if the menstrual cycle were divided into two phases (preovulatory and postovulatory halves of the menstrual cycle), the results of these published reports would be consistent and indicated that the menstrual cycle may have a significant effect on non-contact ACL injuries. The high-risk interval of suffering non-contact ACL injury is within the preovulatory phase, the injuries clustered surrounding the time period between menses and ovulation (Figure 1). These findings suggested that sex hormones might play a role in the incidence of woman's non-contact ACL injuries. And from these points of view, it was speculated that the high-risk interval of suffering non-contact ACL injury might be the phase with low progesterone level.

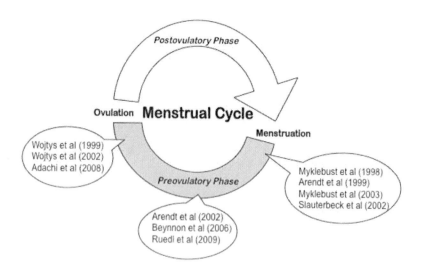

Figure 1. Published studies examining the high-risk interval of the woman's ACL injury during the menstrual cycle

Underlying Factors Affected by the Menstrual Rhythm

The underlying mechanism that increases the likelihood of sustaining an ACL injury during the preovulatory phase of the menstrual cycle has not been determined. There are multiple indications that ACL tissue metabolism, ACL laxity, neuromuscular factors, as well as premenstrual symptoms, may fluctuate during the menstrual cycle.

ACL tissue metabolism

Changes in the ACL tissue properties during the menstrual cycle could be a possible contributor to female ACL injuries. It is known that female sex hormones have a widespread effect on the growth and development of bone, muscle, and connective tissues [13,19,36]. Estrogen, progesterone, relaxin and testosterone receptors present in human ACL tissue. Liu et al. [27] have demonstrated the presence of both estrogen and progesterone receptors in human ACL tissue, suggesting that female sex hormones may have an effect on the structure and composition of the ligament. Yu et al. [49,50] examined the effects of varying doses of estrogen and progesterone on fibroblast metabolism in cell cultures of the human ACL. They suggested that acute increase in sex hormone concentrations across the menstrual cycle might influence ACL metabolism and collagen synthesis. Sex hormones have also been reported to affect tensile properties of ACL [39], but other authors found no significant difference in maximum force, stiffness, energy to failure, or failure site of ACLs in sheep [44]. Recent reports indicated that estrogen and its receptors in fact do not affect ACL mechanical properties [46]. Influences of sex hormone on mechanical properties of ligament tissues have been only studied in animal models. Further research is needed to better establish the influence of sex hormones on the ACL tissue properties.

ACL laxity

Some studies identified the cyclic increases in knee laxity during the normal menstrual cycle [10,20,41,42]. However, recent studies have shown that there is no correlation between the menstrual cycle and knee laxity measurement [6,11,21,24,43,45]. The influence of female hormone cycle on ACL laxity has been inconclusive. The meta-analysis by Zazulak et al. [51] specifically stated that 6 of 9 prospective cohort studies did not show any correlation between laxity and menstrual cycle. The other 3 studies that observed laxity differences between cycle phases reported increased laxity during the post-ovulatory phases relative to the pre-ovulatory phases. Interestingly, the high-risk interval of suffering non-contact ACL injury is within the pre-ovulatory half of the cycle, when the ACL would be less lax or demonstrate greater stiffness. This contradictory relationship between the pre-ovulatory phase laxity and injury findings may be further evidence that cycle dependent changes in hormone concentrations may not consistently influence knee laxity, or possibly that more injuries occur when the ligament is stiffer rather than more lax. The implications of cyclic changes in anterior knee laxity on ACL injury risk have yet to be explored.

Neuromuscular factors

There are several suggested mechanisms for the higher rate of women's ACL injury, although the neuromuscular factor seems to be the most important. Neuromuscular control refers to unconscious activation of the dynamic restraints surrounding a joint in response to sensory stimuli. The neuromuscular system generates movement and determines biomechanics of playing actions. Many athletic maneuvers, such as running, jumping, and cutting, are inherently unstable and require neuromuscular control to maintain stability and improve performance. Hormonal influences on neuromuscular control of the joints of the lower extremity could be an underlying mechanism for higher rates of woman's ACL injury. Recently, gender differences related to neuromuscular control have been also suggested as a potential cause of ACL injury risk in female athletes [18,22,52]. Neuromuscular function seems to also be affected by sex hormones. During the ovulatory phase, there was an increase in quadriceps strength, a decrease in muscle relaxiation time, and an increase in muscle fatigability in young healthy relatively sedentary females [38]. Sex hormones also decrease motor coordination [34] and have effects on isokinetic strength, anaerobic and aerobic capacity, and high-intensity endurance in female athletes [26]. However, Chaudhari et al. [8] investigated knee and hip loading patterns in the menstrual cycle and concluded that variations of the menstrual cycle do not directly affect knee or hip joint loading during jumping and landing task. The authors suggested that the gender difference in ACL injury rates is more likely attributable to persistent difference in strength, neuromuscular coordination, or ligament properties because knee and hip joint loading is unaffected by cyclic variations in hormone levels. The cyclic changes in the measurements of neuromuscular performances across the menstrual cycle have been still equivocal in the literatures. Future research is also needed in this area.

Premenstrual symptoms

The high frequency of several types of menstrual dysfunction during the cycle is observed in female athletes and there is substantial variability that exists among individuals. It is also well known and accepted that certain women experience several symptoms or discomfort during the pre-menstrual and menstrual period [5,26,37]. These symptoms may be defined as when a woman has symptoms that begin at the time of ovulation or thereafter and improve significantly with the onset of menstruation and have resolved by the conclusion of the bleed [31]. Some studies suggested that pre-menstrual and menstrual symptoms affect the athletic performance and neuromuscular control, and may increase the risk of musculoskeletal injuries [14,15,28,30,31]. Friden et al [14] reported that women with premenstrual symptoms have significantly greater postural sway compared with women without cyclical symptoms. In the subsequent study [15], the same group detected menstrual phase difference in postural control in women with cyclical premenstrual symptoms and suggested the possible relationship to the increased injury rate and psychomotor slowing in the liteal phase in women with premenstrual symptoms. Adachi et al [1] investigated the relationship of the menstrual cycle phase to non-contact ACL injuries in teenaged female athletes. They demonstrated a significant increase in non-contact ACL injuries during ovulatory phase but indicated that the subjective activity level during the menstrual cycle and the premenstrual and menstrual symptoms might not affect the likelihood of the injuries. The implications of these symptoms during the menstrual cycle on ACL injury risk in female athletes have not been clarified.

CONCLUSION

This review of the literature indicates that female athletes may be more predisposed to ACL injuries during the preovulatory phase of the menstrual cycle. Intervention programs targeted toward this phase of the menstrual cycle may be effective to reduce the incidence of women's ACL injuries. The underlying mechanism that increases the likelihood of sustaining an ACL injury during the preovulatory phase of the menstrual cycle has not been elucidated. Although sex-based hormone cycling may play a role in the increased rate of ACL injury in women over men, this role may lie in a more complex interaction between several risk factors. Studies focus on an isolated risk factor may not explain the relationship between the normal hormonal fluctuations during the menstrual cycle and the likelihood of non-contact ACL injury in female athletes. Future study should aim to examine the interrelationship between different risk factors for non-contact ACL injuries in female athletes. Further investigations would be expected clinicians and researchers to determine the mechanisms of the likelihood of the woman's non-contact ACL injuries and to develop treatment modalities to aid in the prevention of these injuries.

REFERENCES

[1]   Adachi, N; Nawata, K; Maeta, M; Kurozawa, Y. Relationship of menstrual cycle phase to anterior cruciate ligament injuries in teenaged female athletes. *Arch Orthop Trauma Surg*, 2008, 128, 473-478.

[2]   Alentorn-Geli, E; Myer, GD; Slivers, HJ; Samitier, G; Romero, D; Lazaro-Haro, C; Cugat, R. Prevention of non-contact anterior cruciate ligament injuries in soccer players. Part 1: Mechanisms of injury and underlying risk factors. *Knee Surg Sports Traumatol Arthrosc*, 2009, 17, 705-729.

[3]   Arendt, E; Agel, J; Dick, R. Anterior cruciate ligament injury patterns among collegiate men and women. *J Athl Train*, 1999, 34, 86-92.

[4]   Arendt, E; Bershadsky, B; Agel, J. Periodicity of noncontact anterior cruciate ligament injuries during the menstrual cycle. *J Gend Specif Med*, 2002, 5(2), 19-26.

[5]   Backstrom, T; Baird, DT; Bancroft, J; Bixo, M; Hammarback, S; Sanders, D; Smith, S; Zetterlund, B. Endocrinological aspects of cyclical mood changes during the menstrual cycle or the premenstrual syndrome. *J Psychosomatic Obset Gynaecol*, 1983, 2(1), 8-20.

[6]   Beynnon, BD; Berstein, IM; Belisle, A; Brattbakk, B; Devanny, P; Risinger, R; Durant, D. The effect of estradiol and progesterone on knee and ankle joint laxity. *Am J Sports Med*, 2005, 33(9), 1298-1304.

[7]   Beynnon, BD; Johnson, RJ; Braun, S; Sargent, M; Berstein, IM; Skelly, JM; Vacek, PM. The relationship between menstrual cycle phase and anterior cruciate ligament injury. A case control study of recreational alpine skiers. *Am J Sports Med*, 2006, 34(5), 757-764.

[8]   Chaudhari, AMW; Lindenfeld, TN; Andriacchi, TP; Hewett, TE; Riccobene, J; Myer, GD; Noyes, FR. Knee and hip loading patterns at different phases in the menstrual cycle. *Am J Sports Med*, 2007, 35(5), 793-800.

[9]   Constantini, NW; Dubnov, G; Lebrun, CM. The menstrual cycle and sports performance. *Clin Sports Med*, 2005, e51-e82.

[10]   Deie, M; Sakamaki, Y; Sumen, Y; Urabe, Y; Ikuta, Y. Anterior knee laxity in young women varies with their menstrual cycle. *Int Orthop*, 2002, 26,154-156.

[11]   Eiling, E; Bryant, AL; Peterson, W; Murphy, A; Hohmann, E. Effect of menstrual-cycle hormone fluctuations on musculotendinous stiffness and knee joint laxity. *Knee Surg Sports Traumatol Arthrosc*, 2007, 15, 126-

132.

[12] Espey, LL; Halim, IA. Characteristics and control of the normal menstrual cycle. *Obstet Gynecol Clin North Am*, 1990, 17(2), 275-298.

[13] Fischer, GM. Comparison of collagen dynamics in different tissues under the influence of estradiol. *Endocrinology*, 1973, 93, 1216-1218.

[14] Friden, C; Hirschberg, AL; Saartok, T; Backstrom, T; Leanderson, J; Renstrom, P. The influence of premenstrual symptom on postural balance and kinesthesia during the menstrual cycle. *Gynecol Endocrinol*, 2003, 17(6), 433-439.

[15] Friden, C; Ramsey, DK; Backstrom, T; Benoit, DL; Saartok, T; Hirschberg, AL. Altered postural control during the luteal phase in women with premenstrual symptoms. *Neuroendocrinology*, 2005, 81(3), 150-157.

[16] Friden, C; Hirschberg, AL; Saartok, T; Renstrom, P. Knee joint kinaesthesia and neuromuscular coordination during three phases of the menstrual cycle in moderately active women. *Knee Surg Sports Traumatol Arthrosc*, 2006, 14(4), 383-389.

[17] Grnan, LP; Bahr, R; Steindal, K; Furnes, O; Engebretsen, L. Development of a national cruciate ligament surgery registry: the Norwegian National Knee Ligament Registry. *Am J Sport Med*, 2008, 36(2), 308-315.

[18] Griffin, LA; Albohm, MJ; Arendt, EA; Bahr, R; Beynnon, BD; DeMaio M; Dick, RW; Engebretsen, L; Garrett, WE; Hannafin, JA; Hewett, TE; Huston, LJ; Ireland, ML; Johnson, RJ; Lephart, S; Mandelbaum, BR; Mann, BJ; Marks, PH; Marshall, SW; Myklebust, G; Noyes, FR; Powers, C; Shields, C; Shultz, SJ; Silvers, H; Slauterbeck, J; Taylor, DC; Teitz, CC; Wojtys, EM; Yu, B. Understanding and preventing noncontact anterior cruciate ligament injuries. A review of the Hunt Valley II Meeting, January 2005. *Am J Sports Med*, 2006, 34(9), 1512-1532.

[19] Hama, H; Yamamuro, T; Takeda, T. Experimental studies on connective tissue of the capsular ligament. Influences of aging and sex hormones. *Acta Orthop Scand*, 1976, 47(5), 473-479.

[20] Heitz, NA; Eisenman, PA; Beck, CL; Walker, JA. Hormonal changes throughout the menstrual cycle and increased anterior cruciate ligament laxity in females. *J Athl Train*, 1999, 34(2), 144-149.

[21] Hertel, J; Williams, NI; Olmsted-Kramer, LC; Leidy, HJ; Putukian, M. Neuromuscular performance and knee laxity do not change across the menstrual cycle in female athletes. *Knee Surg Sports Traumatol*

Arthrosc, 2006, 14, 817-822.

[22] Hewett, TE; Myer, GD; Ford, KR. Anterior cruciate ligament injuries in female athletes. Part 1, mechanisms and risk factors. *Am J Sports Med*, 2006, 34(2), 299-311.

[23] Hewett, TE; Zazulak, BT; Myer, GD. Effect of the menstrual cycle on anterior cruciate ligament injury risk. A systematic review. *Am J Sports Med*, 2007, 35(4), 659-668.

[24] Karageanes, SJ; Blackburn, K; Vangelos, ZA. The association of the menstrual cycle with the laxity of the anterior cruciate ligament in adolescent female athletes. *Clin Sports Med*, 2000, 10, 162-168.

[25] Landgren, BM; Unden, AL; Diczfalusy, E. Hormonal profile of the cycle in 68 normally menstruating women. *Acta Endcrinol*, 1980, 94, 89-98.

[26] Lebrun, CM. The effect of the phase of the menstrual cycle and the birth control pill on athletic performance. *Clin Sports Med*, 1994, 13(2), 419-441.

[27] Liu, SH; Al-Shaikh, R; Panossian, V; Yang, R; Nelson, SD; Soleiman, N, Finerman, GAM; Lane, JM. Primary immunolocalization of estrogen and progesterone target cells in the human anterior cruciate ligament. *J Orthop Res.*, 1996, 14(4), 526-533.

[28] Lloyd, T; Triantafyllou, SJ; Baker, ER; Houts, PS; Whiteside, JA; Kalenak, A; Stumpf, PG. Women athletes with menstrual irregularity have increased musculoskeletal injuries. *Med Sci Sports Exerc.*, 1986, 18(4), 374-379.

[29] Malone, TR; Hardaker, WT; Garrett, WE; Feagin, JA; Bassett, FH. Durhan. Relationship of gender to anterior cruciate ligament injuries in intercollegiate basketball players. *J South Orthop Assoc.*, 1993, 2(1), 36-39.

[30] Moller-Nielson, J; Hammar, M. Women's soccer injuries in relation to the menstrual cycle and oral contraceptive use. *Med Sci Sports Exerc.*, 1989, 21(2), 126-129.

[31] Moller-Nielson, J; Hammar, M. Sports injuries and oral contraceptive use. Is there a relationship? *Sports Med*, 1991, 12(3), 152-161.

[32] Myklebust, G; Maehlum, S; Holm, I; Bahr, R. A prospective cohort studies of anterior cruciate ligament injuries in elite Norwegian team handball. *Scand J Med Sci Sports*, 1998, 8, 149-153.

[33] Myklebust, G; Engebretsen, L; Braekken, IH; Skjolberg, A; Olsen, OE; Bahr, R. Prevention of anterior cruciate ligament injuries in female team handball players: a prospective intervention study over three seasons. *Clin J Sport Med*, 2003, 13, 71-78.

[34] Posthuma, BW; Bass, MJ; Bull, SB; Nisker, JA. Detecting changes in functional ability in women with premenstrual syndrome. *Am J Obstet Gynecol*, 1987, 156, 275-278.

[35] Ruedl, G; Ploner, P; Linortner, I; Schranz, A; Fink, C; Sommersacher, R; Pocecco, E; Nachbauer, W; Burtscher, M. Are oral contraceptive use and menstrual cycle phase related to anterior cruciate ligament injury risk in female recreational skiers? *Knee Surg Sports Traumatol Arthrosc*, 2009, Mar 31 [On-line].

[36] Samuel, CS; Butkus, A; Coghlan, JP; Bateman, JF. The effect of relaxin on collagen metabolism in the nonpregnant rat pubic symphysis: the influence of estrogen and progesterone in regulating relaxin activity. *Endocrinology*, 1996, 137(9), 3884-3890.

[37] Sanborn, CF. Menstrual dysfunction in the female athlete. In: Teiz CC (eds) Scientific Foundations of Sports Medicine. BC Decker, *Philadelphia Pa*, 1989, 117-134

[38] Sarwer, R; Beltran, NB; Rutherford, OM. Changes in muscle strength, relaxiation rate and fatiguability during the human menstrual cycle. *J Physiol*, 1996, 493, 267-272.

[39] Slauterbeck, JR; Clevenger, C; Lundberg, W; Burchfield, DM. Estrogen level alters the failure load of the rabbit anterior cruciate ligament. *J Orthop Res.*, 1999, 17, 405-408.

[40] Slauterbeck, JR; Fuzie, SF; Smith, MP; Clark, RJ; Xu KT; Starch, DW; Hardy, DM. The menstrual cycle, sex hormones, and anterior cruciate ligament injury. *J Athl Train*, 2002, 37(3), 275-280.

[41] Shultz, SJ; Kirk, SE; Johnson, ML; Sander, TC; Perrin, DH. Relationship between sex hormones and anterior knee laxity across the menstrual cycle. *Med Sci Sports Exerc.*, 2004, 36, 1165-1174.

[42] Shultz, SJ; Sander, TC; Kirk, SE; Perrin, DH. Sex differences in knee joint laxity change across the female menstrual cycle. *J Sports Med Phys Fitnessi* 2005, 45(4), 594-603.

[43] Shultz, SJ; Gansneder, BM; Sander, TC; Kirk, SE; Perrin, DH. Absolute serum hormone levels predict the magnitude of change in anterior knee laxity across the menstrual cycle. *J Orthop Res.*, 2006 Feb, 24(2), 124-131.

[44] Strickland, SM; Belknap, TW; Turner, SA; Wright, TM; Hannafin, JA. Lack of hormonal influence on mechanical properties of sheep knee ligaments *Am J Sports Med*, 2003, 31, 210-215.

[45] Van Lunen, BL; Roberts, J; Branch, D; Dowling, EA. Association of menstrual-cycle hormone changes with anterior cruciate ligament laxity

measurements. *J Athl Train*, 2003, 38(4), 298-303.

[46]   Warden, SJ; Saxon, LK; Castillo, AB; Turner, CH. Knee ligament mechanical properties are not influenced by estrogen or its receptors. *Am J Physiol Endocrinol Metab*, 2006, 290, E1034-E1040.

[47]   Woitys, EM; Huston, LJ; Lindenfeld, TN; Hewett, TE; Greenfield MLVH. Association between the menstrual cycle and anterior cruciate ligament injuries in female athletes. *Am J Sports Med*, 1998, 26(5), 614-619.

[48]   Woitys, EM; Huston, LJ; Boynton, MD; Spindler, KP; Lindenfeld, TN. The effect of the menstrual cycle on anterior cruciate ligament injuries in women as determined by hormone levels. *Am J Sports Med*, 2002, 30(2), 182-188.

[49]   Yu, WD; Liu, SH; Hatch, JD; Panossian, V; Finerman, GAM. Effect of estrogen on cellular metabolism of the human anterior cruciate ligament. *Clin Orthop Relat Res.*, 1999, 366, 229-238.

[50]   Yu, WD; Panossian, V; Hatch, JD; Liu, SH; Finerman, GAM. Combined effects of estrogen and progesterone on the anterior cruciate ligament. *Clin Orthop Relat Res.*, 2001, 383, 268-281.

[51]   Zuzulak, BT; Paterno, M; Myer, GD; Roman, WA; Hewett, TE. The effects of the menstrual cycle on anterior knee laxity. A systematic review. *Sports Med*, 2006, 36(10), 847-862.

[52]   Zazulak, BT; Hewett, TE; Reeves, NP; Goldberg, MB; Cholewicki, J. The effects of core proprioception on knee injury. A prospective biomechanical-epidemiological study. *Am J Sports Med*, 2007, 35(3), 368-373.

In: Women in Sports
Editors: Amelia S. Halloway pp. 55-76

ISBN: 978-1-61728-161-7
© 2010 Nova Science Publishers, Inc.

Chapter 4

TESTIMONY OF MARCIA D. GREENBERGER, CO-PRESIDENT, NATIONAL WOMEN'S LAW CENTER, BEFORE THE SUBCOMMITTEE ON HIGHER EDUCATION, LIFELONG LEARNING, AND COMPETITIVENESS OF THE HOUSE COMMITTEE ON EDUCATION AND LABOR ON BUILDING ON THE SUCCESS OF 35 YEARS OF TITLE IX

Marcia D. Greenberger

I am Marcia Greenberger, Co-President of the National Women's Law Center. Thank you for the invitation to appear before you today to mark the 35th anniversary of enactment of Title IX of the Education Amendments of 1972 (Title IX), the bedrock federal law that bans sex discrimination in federally funded education programs and activities. On this anniversary, there is much to celebrate; women have made significant progress in education in the last three and one half decades. But the job is not yet finished and the playing field is not yet level; much remains to be done to ensure that women have truly equal access and opportunities in all areas of education.

The Center is a non-profit organization that has worked since 1972 to advance and protect the legal rights of women and girls across the country. The Center focuses on major policy areas of importance to women and their families, including education, employment, health and reproductive rights, and economic security – with particular attention paid to the concerns of low-income women. Founded in the year that Title IX was passed, the Center has devoted much of its resources to ensuring that the promise of Title IX becomes a reality in all aspects of education.

In recognition of this year's anniversary, the Center is today releasing a variety of informational and enforcement materials which I will discuss in my testimony. These include a national survey of 1,000 likely voters that measures support for and understanding of Title IX; an analysis of the athletics complaints filed with, and compliance reviews conducted by, the Department of Education's Office for Civil Rights over the last five years; a legal manual that provides a step-by-step approach to educate those subject to discrimination in athletics, as well as their advocates and attorneys, on how to assert a Title IX claim; and a website designed to enable the public to hold their schools accountable for compliance with the law. These resources are intended to help to realize Title IX's as yet unfulfilled promise of true gender equity in the classrooms and on the playing fields.

Title IX was enacted in 1972 as a broad proscription against discrimination in any federally funded education program or activity. It states simply:

> *No person in the United States shall, on the basis of sex, be excluded from participation in, be denied the benefits of or be subjected to discrimination under any education program or activity receiving Federal financial assistance.*[1]

Title IX applies to all public elementary and secondary schools and to virtually every college and university. It was intended to ensure equal opportunity for women and girls in all aspects of education – from access to higher education, to equal opportunities and fair treatment in elementary and secondary classrooms, to equal chances to participate in athletics programs. In passing Title IX, Congress recognized the critical role that education plays in promoting economic security for women and their families and mandated the broadest scope of protection against sex discrimination in school.

---

[1] Title IX of the Education Amendments of 1972, 20 U.S.C. § 1681 *et seq.*

Congress' vision has borne fruit. Thirty-five years after enactment of the law, we have more female doctors and lawyers. The number of girls going to college has exploded; young women today comprise over half of the undergraduate students in the country, an increase of more than 160% from their representation in 1972.[2] The explicit exclusions of, and quotas for, women in education that were so prevalent 35 years ago have long since disappeared – or at least been driven underground.

In athletics as well, the progress of women and girls has been transformative. When Congress passed Title IX in 1972, fewer than 32,000 women competed in intercollegiate athletics.[3] Women received only 2 percent of schools' athletics budgets, and athletic scholarships for women were nonexistent.[4] Today, the number of college women participating in competitive athletics is now *five times* the pre-Title IX rate. In 2004-05, a record number of 166,728 women competed at the college level, representing 42% of college athletes nationwide.[5]

Title IX has also had a tremendous impact on female athletic opportunities at the high school level. Before Title IX, fewer than 300,000 high school girls played competitive sports.[6] By 2005, the number had climbed to 2.95 million, an increase of almost 900%.[7]

And Title IX has garnered overwhelming public support. The national survey the Center is releasing today confirms that more than eight in ten voters – or 82% of adults - support Title IX.[8] In fact, support for the law is intense, with nearly two-thirds (65%) strongly supporting the law and fewer than one in ten (9%) strongly opposing it. This support crosses the political spectrum;

---

[2] U.S. Department of Education, National Center for Education Statistics (NCES), *The Condition of Education*, table 8-1, *available at http://nces.ed.gov/programs/coe/2007/section1/ table.asp?tableID=672.*

[3] *See* Department of Health, Education, and Welfare, Policy Interpretation, 44 Fed. Reg. at 71419 (1979).

[4] Remarks of Senator Stevens (R-AL), 130 Cong. Rec. S 4601 (daily ed. April 12, 1984).

[5] National Collegiate Athletic Association (NCAA), *1981-82—2004-05 NCAA Sports Sponsorship and Participation Rates Report* 72 (2006).

[6] National Federation of State High School Associations (NFHS), *1971 Sports Participation Survey* (1971).

[7] National Federation of State High School Associations (NFHS), *2005 High School Athletics Participation Survey* 2 (2005).

[8] Memorandum from The Mellman Group, Inc. on Title IX to the National Women's Law Center, 1 (June 8, 2007) (on file with the National Women's Law Center.)

86% of Democratic voters and 78% of Republican and independent voters favor the law.[9]

Moreover, Americans are nearly unanimous in backing those who take action to redress discrimination. Eighty-eight percent of respondents to the survey support girls or their parents taking action to address situations in which girls' high school teams are being treated worse than the boys' teams. This support is consistent across genders and political affiliation.[10]

But despite this progress, significant problems remain. Girls, like their male peers, are dropping out of high school at dangerously high rates. In fact, one in four girls overall, and nearly one in two African American, Hispanic, and Native American female students, fail to graduate with a diploma each year.[1,2] While girls in each racial and ethnic group fare better than boys of the same race or ethnicity, moreover, Black, Hispanic, and American Indian/Alaskan Native female students graduate at significantly lower rates than White and Asian-American males. And tellingly, the consequences for girls who fail to graduate from high school are profound and deeply disturbing. Female dropouts are at much greater risk than their male peers of being unemployed. They make significantly lower wages and are more likely to rely on public support programs to provide for their families.

Another example of the pervasive barriers that remain can be found in career and technical education (CTE). The divide between boys and girls in CTE has barely narrowed since Congress passed Title IX 35 years ago. Just as in the 1 970s, high school girls are the vast majority of those who enroll in traditionally female courses, such as cosmetology and child care, while boys make up all but a tiny percentage of the students in traditionally male fields such as auto mechanics and construction and repair. This sex segregation in the nation's vocational classrooms - and the relegation of girls to traditionally female programs - has deep impact on the earning power and job prospects of the young women who graduate from these programs. Girls who take up traditionally female occupations can expect to earn half - or less - what they

---

[9] *Id.*

[10] *Id.* at 2.

[1] Greene, J. and Winters, M., *Leaving Boys Behind: Public High School Graduation Rates,* Manhattan Institute Civic Report 48 (2006).

[2] Orfield, G., et al., *Losing Our Future: How Minority Youth are Being Left Behind by the Graduation Rate Crisis,* Cambridge, MA: The Civil Rights Project at Harvard University. Contributors: Urban Institute, Advocates for Children of New York, and The Civil Society Institute (2004).

could make if they went into traditionally male fields like auto repair, welding, or engineering.[13]

As my colleagues on the panel today will discuss, similar problems plague women in science, technology, engineering and math – the STEM disciplines. And as you will also hear, sexual harassment remains all too widespread, creating hostile educational environments for far too many young women at every level of education. All of these are areas in which Congress must act – to ensure that the strongest possible legal standards exist to protect the civil rights of young women; to mandate that the Department of Education and other Title IX enforcement agencies take the proactive and comprehensive steps necessary to enforce the law; and to ensure that Title IX's promise of true gender equity becomes a reality.

For my testimony today, I would like to focus on Title IX's impact on athletics and the steps that still must be taken to create a level playing field for our nation's daughters.

I. WOMEN AND GIRLS STILL FACE PERSISTENT DISCRIMINATION IN ATHLETICS

Notwithstanding the extraordinary gains that women have made, female participation in intercollegiate sports remains *below pre-Title IX male participation:* while 170,384 men played college sports in 197 1-1972, only 166,728 women played college sports in 2004-05.[14] In addition, participation opportunities as well as resources for women's athletic programs continue to lag behind men's. Women receive only 43% of the opportunities to participate in college sports,[15] even though they comprise 55% of today's undergraduates.[16] In Division I, they receive only 45% of athletics scholarships, 37% of athletics operating expenses, and 32% of the dollars spent on recruiting.[17]

---

[13] *See* National Women's Law Center, *Tools of the Trade: Using the Law To Address Sex Segregation In High School Career and Technical Education* (2005), *available at* http://www.nwlc.org/pdf/NWLCToolsoftheTrade05.pdf.

[14] *See* Department of Health, Education, and Welfare, Policy Interpretation, 44 Fed. Reg. at 71419 (1979).

[15] National Collegiate Athletic Association (NCAA), 1981-82—2004-05 *NCAA Sports Sponsorship and Participation Rates Report* 72 (2006).

[16] National Collegiate Athletic Association (NCAA) *2003-04 Gender-Equity Report* 12 (2007).

[17] *Id.* at 25.

The persistence of discrimination is further illustrated by recent research. The survey being released by the Center today shows that 22% of respondents – a sample that represents more than 50 million adults -- were aware of recent situations in which girls' sports teams in high school or college were being treated worse than boys' teams.[18] Moreover, the Center has just concluded a new examination of the athletics complaints filed with, and compliance reviews conducted by, the Department of Education's Office for Civil Rights over the last five years. This review reveals that 35 years after the enactment of Title IX, women are still given fewer opportunities than males to participate in sports, and, when they do play, are treated like second- class citizens in the facilities, equipment, coaching, publicity and other support services that they receive. Here are some of the key findings of the Center's report, *Barriers to Fair Play*:[19]

- **Discrimination against girls and women in sports remains widespread.** There were 416 athletics complaints filed with OCR between January 1, 2002 and December 31, 2006 – likely just a fraction of the number of complaints that were raised informally with schools during that period. The OCR complaints challenged discrimination against girls or women 11 times more frequently than they claimed discrimination against males, demonstrating concretely that the playing field is still far from level for female athletes.

- **Schools' second-class treatment of female athletes, even when they are given a chance to play, is a particular concern.** While more than one-quarter of the complaints overall challenged schools' failures to provide sufficient participation opportunities for girls and women, more than half – 54% - challenged inequitable treatment of girls' or women's teams once female athletes were allowed to play. Among complaints filed by or on behalf of girls, moreover, fully 60% of the allegations concerned inequities in treatment of female teams. And many of the treatment complaints – particularly those concerning disparities between girls' softball and boys' baseball teams, such as in

---

[18] The Mellman Group, Inc., Title IX Survey, Conducted May 22-24, 2007 1 (on file with the National Women's Law Center).

[19] Each of the following points is drawn from the National Women's Law Center's report *Barriers to Fair Play*, *available at* http://www.nwlc.org.

the quality of softball versus baseball fields – identified blatant and egregious inequities that had persisted for many years.

- **Coaches fear retaliation if they complain, so the burden typically falls on students and their parents to protest discrimination.** Although coaches have greater access to information and are often in the best position to perceive and challenge discrimination, coaches filed only just shy of 8% of the 416 complaints made during the relevant period. Tellingly, a full 50% of those complaints alleged retaliation in addition to other forms of discrimination against the coaches and their female athletes.

- **Discrimination complaints filed by or on behalf of female athletes were far more likely to be meritorious enough to secure changes than complaints filed by or on behalf of male athletes.** Schools made changes to their athletics programs in response to complaints filed by or on behalf of female athletes at close to five times the rate at which they made changes in response to complaints filed by or on behalf of male athletes. As a corollary, OCR found no violation in almost double the number of complaints filed by men as in complaints filed by women.

In addition to, and reinforcing, the report and survey the National Women's Law Center is issuing today, the Women's Sports Foundation last week released a new report, "Who's Playing College Sports," which includes an analysis revealing the disparities that still exist between men's and women's participation opportunities in intercollegiate sports. These resources all confirm the persistence of discrimination against women and girls on the playing field.

II. OCR ENFORCEMENT EFFORTS HAVE FALLEN SHORT

Significantly, *Barriers to Fair Play* also reveals that OCR has failed to take the proactive steps necessary to combat discrimination in athletics. In some cases, moreover, the agency delayed justice or placed unreasonable burdens on complainants.

In addition to responding to complaints, OCR is responsible for initiating assessments of Title IX compliance by federally funded educational institutions across the country. During the five year period covered by the Center's review, however, OCR initiated only *one* compliance review of a school's athletics program – a record substantially below that of the preceding Administration. Not only has the number of compliance reviews noticeably decreased over the past 6 to 7 years; the focus of those reviews has narrowed considerably. Between 1995 and 2000, OCR annual reports either listed equal opportunity in athletics as a focus of enforcement efforts or provided examples of compliance reviews that addressed athletics. But between 2001 and 2005, no annual reports mentioned athletics as a focus for compliance reviews, and none cited examples of athletics as evidence of successful reviews. Instead, OCR reports for 2003 through 2005 all focus on ensuring that state agencies have designated Title IX coordinators, developed and disseminated antidiscrimination procedures, and implemented grievance procedures. In fact, 50 of 59 compliance reviews between 2002 and 2006 dealt exclusively with these procedural violations.[20]

Strong internal procedures and policies are, of course, essential for schools to adequately address substantive Title IX violations. But the existence of such policies should represent only the beginning of an inquiry about a school's compliance with Title IX's substantive requirements. A school's designation of a Title IX coordinator and the establishment of procedures are necessary but insufficient steps to ensure that real action is being taken to end sex discrimination. OCR's failure to go beyond this superficial examination of a school's policies and practices represents a damaging reduction in its enforcement efforts.

In addition, the resolution of some of the complaints filed in this period was unreasonably delayed in a number of instances; in one case, a complaint languished in the Kansas City regional office for nearly 4 1/2 years. Moreover, OCR sometimes put onerous evidentiary burdens on female athletes filing complaints, for example by refusing to investigate a complaint alleging disparities between a school's softball and baseball teams unless the complainant could produce evidence of overall program violations for all teams.[21] This represents an abdication of OCR's enforcement responsibilities, given that complainants often lack access to the information necessary to evaluate an athletics program overall, and demonstrates the need for strong oversight over OCR's enforcement efforts.

---

[20] National Women's Law Center, *Barriers to Fair Play* (2007).
[21] *Id.*

III. PRIVATE ENFORCEMENT IS NECESSARY TO ENSURE EFFECTIVE PROTECTION OF TITLE IX RIGHTS

The inadequacies of OCR's enforcement point up the importance of educating people about their rights under the law and ensuring that they have the tools and the representation they need to effectively challenge violations of Title IX. In fact, the Center's own experience confirms that individuals can make an enormous difference in leveling the playing field. Here are just a few examples of individuals we have worked with and supported over the past five years:

- As you will later hear from Mr. Jack Mowatt, in 2006 the Prince George's County Public Schools Board of Education approved a county-wide Title IX settlement with the Center to ensure that girls in each of the county's middle and high schools are given equal treatment of their teams and equal opportunities to participate in sports. The settlement resulted after Mr. Mowatt brought attention to the unsafe conditions at county softball fields; as a Washington Post article, *Title IX Deal Transforms Dreams to Fields,* demonstrated during the spring, female athletes in Prince George's County were elated with the improvements the County has already begun to make.
- In 2003, Washington-Lee High School in Arlington, Virginia agreed to take significant steps toward correcting inequities that pervaded the girls' sports program. The settlement resulted after Christine Boehm, a senior and four-year member of the field hockey team, realized there were serious disparities between the treatment of male and female athletes, including the absence of a locker room for female athletes, poorly maintained field hockey fields, and fewer amenities such as permanent scoreboards and covered dugout areas. Ms. Boehm first brought the problems to the school's attention in 2002. The Center, along with the law firm of DLA Piper, negotiated the settlement to remedy the inequalities.
- In 2005, the United States Supreme Court held that Title IX provides protection from retaliation to those who challenge discrimination. In *Jackson v. Birmingham Board of Education,* Roderick Jackson sued the Birmingham Board of Education for firing him as the girls' high school basketball coach after he complained about the inequalities his team endured, including inferior facilities, travel arrangements to

games, amenities, and financial support from the city. Following the Supreme Court ruling, the Board reached an agreement with Coach Jackson in November 2006. He returned to coaching at Jackson-Olin High School and was compensated for his financial losses. Significantly, the Board also agreed to district-wide modifications to their athletics programs to ensure that all of its schools were in compliance with Title IX.

- Earlier this year, the United States Supreme Court denied review in *Communities for Equity v. MHSAA*, in which the lower courts consistently found that the Michigan High School Athletics Association had violated the U.S. Constitution, Title IX and Michigan state law by scheduling six girls' sports, and no boys' sports, in nontraditional and disadvantageous seasons. A group spearheaded by two local parents, Communities for Equity, brought suit to challenge MHSAA's scheduling decisions, which meant that girls across the state had limited opportunities to be seen by college recruiters, to compete for athletic scholarships, and to play club sports. The Supreme Court's denial of review means that justice for Michigan girls should finally be around the corner, when the Association implements a plan that will equalize the seasons in which boys and girls play in the state.

IV. MORE MUST BE DONE TO ENSURE THAT STUDENTS, PARENTS, COACHES AND ADVOCATES HAVE THE TOOLS THEY NEED TO ENFORCE THE LAW

As the examples above illustrate, individuals, including students, parents, coaches and other advocates, have a tremendous ability to make a difference in leveling the playing field for female athletes. But the poll the Center is releasing today shows that they need information and guidance. In the national survey, only 40% of respondents said they knew what steps to take to enforce Title IX.[22] Similarly, *Barriers to Fair Play* reveals that more must be done to educate high school students and parents about their rights. Although female high school athletes file a greater absolute number of complaints than their college-aged counterparts, female college athletes file complaints at

---

[22] Memorandum from The Mellman Group, Inc. on Title IX to the National Women's Law Center, 2 (June 8, 2007) (on file with the National Women's Law Center.)

significantly higher *rates* than high school students. This trend, which likely reflects high school students' lack of knowledge about Title IX or their rights under the law, is particularly troubling because it is most often through participation in sports in their teenage years that girls not only learn life skills but become prepared to play in college and to maintain healthy lifestyles into the future.

In order to provide this education – and in the absence of adequate government enforcement of the law – the Center is today unveiling two new resources designed to enable individuals to effectively assert their rights under Title IX. The first is *Breaking Down Barriers*, a comprehensive manual that takes a step-by-step approach to educate those subject to discrimination in athletics, as well as their advocates and attorneys, on how to assert a Title IX claim. The second is a new website, FairPlayNow.org, which the Center is maintaining with the Women's Sports Foundation and regional partners from around the country including the Women's Law Project in Philadelphia, the California Women's Law Center and the Northwest Women's Law Center. FairPlayNow is designed to provide one-stop shopping for students, parents, coaches, advocates, and attorneys to learn about Title IX, find tools to evaluate their schools' compliance with the law, and use materials that can help them hold their schools accountable for remedying discrimination.

VI. CONGRESS MUST DO MORE TO ENSURE EFFECTIVE PROTECTION FROM SEX DISCRIMINATION

My colleagues today will address some of the ways in which Congressional action is necessary to address the barriers that persist in STEM disciplines and the sexual harassment that continues to limit educational opportunities for far too many young women. With regard to athletics, there are three specific and concrete actions that Congress can, and must, take to ensure effective protection of the law.

First, given the rampant discrimination that still exists, Congress must exercise more oversight over OCR. With its enforcement powers, OCR can effect great changes, but this requires a targeting of resources and a greater commitment to enforce Title IX in all areas of education. Congressional oversight can help to ensure that OCR uses all of the enforcement tools available to it, including compliance reviews and proactive measures like the provision of technical assistance, as well as that OCR applies strong legal standards and seeks effective remedies for discrimination.

Second, Congress can vastly improve the ability to address discrimination at the high school level by passing the High School Athletics Accountability Act. This bipartisan bill, which was introduced in the House by Representatives Louise Slaughter and Shelley Moore Capito, would amend the Elementary and Secondary Education Act of 1965 to direct coeducational elementary and secondary schools to make publicly available information on equality in school athletic programs. The bill would require schools to provide information about the gender breakdown of students who participate in athletics, as well the expenditures the schools make for each team. This information is already required at the college level, and is largely collected, but not disclosed, by high schools. The bill would thus fill a gaping hole in access to information that is necessary to evaluate whether schools are fulfilling their obligations under Title IX and would thereby improve the ability of students, parents and others to ensure enforcement of the law.

Third, Congress must take steps to overturn and limit the Additional Clarification that the Department of Education issued in March 2005 without notice or opportunity for public comment. This new policy is dangerous because it allows schools to show compliance with Title IX's participation requirements simply by sending an email survey to female students and then claiming that a failure to respond indicates a lack of interest in playing sports. The Clarification weakens the law by eliminating schools' obligations to look broadly and proactively at whether they are satisfying women's interest, and threatens to reverse enormous progress women and girls have made in sports since the enactment of Title IX.

CONCLUSION

While much progress has been made over the last 35 years under Title IX, many battles still must be fought to eradicate sex discrimination in education and enable women and girls to realize their full potential. Women and girls still face unacceptable and unlawful barriers to athletic opportunity, which continue to contribute to the "corrosive and unjustified discrimination against women" that Title IX was intended to eliminate.[23] We must use this anniversary to recommit ourselves to making the letter and the spirit of the Title IX law a reality across all areas of education.

---

[23] 118 Cong. Rec.5803 (1972) (remarks of Sen. Bayh).

In: Women in Sports   ISBN: 978-1-61728-161-7
Editors: Amelia S. Halloway pp. 77-80   © 2010 Nova Science Publishers, Inc.

Chapter 5

TESTIMONY OF JACK MOWATT, COMMISSIONER, MARYLAND-DC AMATEUR SOFTBALL ASSOCIATION, BEFORE THE SUBCOMMITTEE ON HIGHER EDUCATION, LIFELONG LEARNING, AND COMPETITIVENESS OF THE HOUSE COMMITTEE ON EDUCATION AND LABOR ON BUILDING ON THE SUCCESS OF 35 YEARS OF TITLE IX

Jack Mowatt

Chairman Hinojosa, Ranking Member Keller, and members of the Committee, thank you for inviting me to testify before you today. I would like to share with you my story of the gender equity problems that I saw in the girls' athletics programs in Prince George's County, Maryland and how those problems were resolved in a way that could be replicated in other communities across the country.

I have been an active softball umpire in the Washington, D.C. metropolitan area since 1968 and have seen many softball fields in Maryland. Over the years, I became more and more concerned about many of the safety issues that I saw on the girls' high school softball fields in Prince George's County, Maryland. Several years ago during a game, I thought: *These young women deserve more than this.* It has been my belief that athletes who play on good fields play better and enjoy the game much more.

I talked to a fellow umpire who has also been officiating for a number of years, and we decided to go around to the schools in Prince George's County and take pictures of the safety hazards at the girls' fields and see if we could get the school district to make improvements to the fields. Our main concern was the unsafe conditions to which these young women were exposed on their school softball fields. At first, I did not think of the problems as gender equity problems, but now I realize that by not taking care of the softball fields, the county was sending a message to girls that their sports are not as important.

Our photographs of the fields showed problems that go beyond safety concerns. The girls' softball fields did not have basic things that the boys' fields had, such as benches for the team and fencing to protect them. For example, at Largo High School, the boys' baseball field there had perimeter fencing, dug outs and a scoreboard. The girls' softball field had none of those amenities.

After we had taken pictures of every high school softball field in Prince George's County, we presented the County Athletic Director with the photographs and asked him to make improvements to the girls' fields. We also requested help from the former superintendent. Unfortunately, after numerous conversations, nothing was done to improve the girls' fields.

After a year, when we saw that Prince George's County was not responding, one of the softball coaches and I contacted the National Women's Law Center in 2003. Together with the Center, we did a more comprehensive investigation of the treatment of female athletes as compared to male athletes in Prince George's County. We found serious problems in the way girls' teams were treated, including in the number of participation opportunities offered to girls and the amount of money the school district spends on girls' sports.

The Center sent a letter to attorneys for the Prince George's County Public Schools in the fall of 2004 describing all the ways in which girls were not being treated fairly and reminding the county of its Title IX obligations. Fortunately, the county stepped up to the plate and recognized that it needed to make changes. Over the next year and a half, the Center, together with attorneys from the D.C. office of Steptoe & Johnson, LLP, negotiated an agreement that includes all public middle and high schools in the county and requires equal treatment for girls in opportunities to practice and play, funding and facilities, and many other areas. Some of the details include:

By the beginning of the 2007 softball season, the Board had to improve its softball fields and conditions of play, which at some schools required that it install backstops and fencing to protect players and fans from balls, eliminate jagged edges around fencing, and make sure that fields are free of gaping holes and other safety hazards. These small changes, which the Board has already made, have led girls playing softball to feel like for the first time, they are important. (See Josh Barr, "Title IX Deal Transforms Dreams to Fields," Wash. Post, March 22, 2007, at E7.)

By the beginning of the 2008 softball season, the Board will make additional improvements to the softball fields to provide girls with the same amenities that are already provided to boys' baseball teams. In some cases this will include covered dugouts, scoreboards and bleachers.

Beyond softball, the Board agreed to provide equal funding for boys' and girls' sports and to make sure that outside fundraising does not create inequalities between boys' and girls' programs. The Board will also provide girls' and boys' teams with equal facilities and the male and female athletes will receive equal amounts – and equal quality – of publicity.

Finally, the people of Prince George's County will be able to hold the Board to its word that it will provide these equal opportunities to its male and female students.

The Agreement requires that the Board regularly evaluate its athletics program and its compliance with the Agreement, and that it make its reports public. A copy of the agreement is attached to my testimony.

I am so glad that the Board of Education agreed to do the right thing and correct these problems. Their actions send a strong message to girls that they matter just as much as boys. And providing girls with equal opportunities to play sports is an investment in their future. Studies show that girls who play sports have higher grades, are less likely to drop out and have higher graduation rates than those who do not play sports. Athletes are less likely to smoke or use drugs, and female athletes have lower rates of both sexual activity and pregnancy than females who do not play sports. Playing sports also decreases a young woman's chance of developing heart disease, breast cancer and depression. (See National Women's Law Center, "The Battle for Gender Equity in Athletics in Elementary and Secondary Schools," June 2007, available at http://www.nwlc.org/details.cfm?id=2735&section=athletics.)

Unfortunately, I learned that the problems we found in Prince George's County are not unique. Title IX turns 35 this week, and while women and girls have come a long way since the law was passed in 1972, there is lots of work still to do. For example, there are many other reports of girls across the country playing on run-down, bare bones softball fields, while boys play on fields fit for minor league baseball teams.

I am so glad that the Board agreed to make changes that will benefit girls throughout Prince George's County and I hope school districts nationwide follow the school board's lead. Several years ago I decided that the conditions were too unsafe for me to continue umpiring in the County. But because of this agreement, I decided to go back to being an umpire and I am so excited to see the changes first hand. Thank you.

In: Women in Sports   ISBN: 978-1-61728-161-7
Editors: Amelia S. Halloway pp. 81-87   © 2010 Nova Science Publishers, Inc.

Chapter 6

FITNESS AND BONE HEALTH FOR WOMEN: THE SKELETAL RISK OF OVERTRAINING

National Institute of Health

Are you exercising too much? Eating too little? Have your menstrual periods stopped or become irregular? If so, you may be putting yourself at high risk for several serious problems that could affect your health, your ability to remain active, and your risk for injuries. You also may be putting yourself at risk for developing osteoporosis, a disease in which bone density is decreased, leaving your bones vulnerable to fracture (breaking).

WHY IS MISSING MY PERIOD SUCH A BIG DEAL?

Some athletes see amenorrhea (the absence of menstrual periods) as a sign of successful training. Others see it as a great answer to a monthly inconvenience. And some young women accept it blindly, not stopping to think of the consequences. But missing your periods is often a sign of decreased estrogen levels. And lower estrogen levels can lead to osteoporosis, a disease in which your bones become brittle and more likely to break.

Usually, bones don't become brittle and break until women are much older. But some young women, especially those who exercise so much that their periods stop, develop brittle bones, and may start to have fractures at a very early age. Some 20-year-old female athletes have been said to have the bones of an 80-year-old woman. Even if bones don't break when you're young, low estrogen levels during the peak years of bone-building, the preteen and teen years, can affect bone density for the rest of your life. And studies show that bone growth lost during these years may never be regained.

Broken bones don't just hurt—they can cause lasting physical malformations. Have you noticed that some older women and men have stooped postures? This is not a normal sign of aging. Fractures from osteoporosis have left their spines permanently altered.

Overtraining can cause other problems besides missed periods. If you don't take in enough calcium and vitamin D (among other nutrients), bone loss may result. This may lead to decreased athletic performance, decreased ability to exercise or train at desired levels of intensity or duration, and increased risk of injury.

WHO IS AT RISK FOR THESE PROBLEMS?

"I was training really hard—all the time. Finally, my parents made me quit the cross country team ...I was eating almost nothing, training with a stress fracture... I trained even when my body ached. I thought the pain, the headaches, and the missed menstrual periods were normal. I thought that was how a 'champion' was supposed to feel and train. I was proud of myself for being so thin and disciplined and losing all the 'baby fat' I had carried throughout junior high school. My friends all said, "Gosh, you have lost so much weight!" But I wasn't in control. After my parents made me quit the team and took me to get help, I realized that my training regimen was not normal or healthy. I realized that I was hurting myself and that I did not have to be obsessive about my weight, eating habits, and exercise in order to be attractive. I still exercise now, and I watch what I eat, but I am much more relaxed, healthier (my doctor says!), and happier. I have more energy—and more fun. I don't have to set any records anymore, and I am a champion anyway!"

—An athlete who recovered from problems associated with overtraining and missed periods.

Girls and women who engage in rigorous exercise regimens or who try to lose weight by restricting their eating are at risk for these health problems. They may include serious athletes, "gym rats" (who spend considerable time and energy working out), and girls and women who believe "you can never be too thin."

How Can I Tell if Someone I Know, Train with, or Coach May Be at Risk for Bone Loss, Fracture, and Other Health Problems?

Here are some signs to look for:

missed or irregular menstrual periods
extreme or "unhealthy-looking" thinness
extreme or rapid weight loss
behaviors that reflect frequent dieting, such as eating very little, not eating
    in front of others, trips to the bathroom following meals, preoccupa-
    tion with thinness or weight, focus on low-calorie and diet foods,
    possible increase in the consumption of water and other no- and low-
    calorie foods and beverages, possible increase in gum chewing, limit-
    ing diet to one food group, or eliminating a food group
frequent intense bouts of exercise (e.g., taking an aerobics class, then run-
    ning 5 miles, then swimming for an hour, followed by weight-lifting)
an "I can't miss a day of exercise/practice" attitude
an overly anxious preoccupation with an injury
exercising despite illness, inclement weather, injury, and other conditions
    that might lead someone else to take the day off
an unusual amount of self-criticism or self-dissatisfaction
indications of significant psychological or physical stress, including de-
    pression, anxiety or nervousness, inability to concentrate, low levels
    of self-esteem, feeling cold all the time, problems sleeping, fatigue,
    injuries, and constantly talking about weight.

How Can I Make Needed Changes to Improve My Bone Health?

If you recognize some of these signs in yourself, the best thing you can do is to make your diet more healthful. That includes consuming enough calories to support your activity level. If you've missed periods, it's best to check with a doctor to make it's not a sign of some other problem and to get his or her help as you work toward a more healthy balance of food and exercise. Also, a doctor can help you take steps to protect your bones from further damage.

WHAT CAN I DO IF I SUSPECT A FRIEND MAY HAVE SOME OF THESE SIGNS?

First, be supportive. Approach your friend or teammate carefully, and be sensitive. She probably won't appreciate a lecture about how she should be taking better care of herself. But maybe you could share a copy of this fact sheet with her or suggest that she talk to a trainer, coach, or doctor about the symptoms she's experiencing.

MY FRIEND DRINKS A LOT OF DIET SODAS. SHE SAYS THIS HELPS KEEP HER TRIM

Girls and women who may be dieting often drink diet sodas rather than milk. Yet, milk and other dairy products are a good source of calcium, an essential ingredient for healthy bones. Drinking sodas instead of milk can be a problem, especially during the teen years when rapid bone growth occurs. If you (or your friend) find yourself drinking a lot of sodas, try drinking half as many sodas each day, and gradually add more milk and dairy products to your diet. A frozen yogurt shake can be an occasional low-fat, tasty treat. Or try a fruit smoothie made with frozen yogurt, fruit, or calcium-enriched orange juice.

FOR FITNESS INSTRUCTORS AND TRAINERS

It's important for you to be aware of problems associated with bone loss in today's active young women. As an instructor or trainer, you are the one who sees, leads, and perhaps even evaluates the training sessions and performances of your clients. You may know best when something seems to be amiss. You also may be the best person to help a zealous female exerciser recognize that she is putting herself at risk for bone loss and other health problems and that she should establish new goals.

> *Trainers and instructors also should be aware of the implicit or explicit messages they send. Health, strength, and fitness should be emphasized, rather than thinness. Use caution when advising female clients to lose weight. And, if such a recommendation is deemed necessary, knowledgeable personnel should offer education and assistance about proper and safe weight management. As an instructor or trainer, it's best to maintain a professional rapport with your clients, so they can feel comfortable approaching you with concerns about their exercise training programs, appropriate exercise goals and time lines, body image and nutrition issues, as well as more personal problems regarding eating practices and menstruation.*

MY COACH AND I THINK I SHOULD LOSE JUST A LITTLE MORE WEIGHT. I WANT TO BE ABLE TO EXCEL AT MY SPORT!

Years ago, it was not unusual for coaches to encourage athletes to be as thin as possible for many sports (e.g., dancing, gymnastics, figure skating, swimming, diving, and running). However, many coaches now realize that being too thin is unhealthy and can negatively affect performance. It's important to exercise and watch what you eat. However, it's also important to develop and maintain healthy bones and bodies. Without these, it will not matter how fast you can run, how thin you are, or how long you exercise each day. Balance is the key!

I'M STILL NOT CONVINCED. IF MY BONES BECOME BRITTLE, SO WHAT? WHAT'S THE WORST THING THAT COULD HAPPEN TO ME?

Brittle bones may not sound as scary as a fatal or rare disease. The fact is that osteoporosis can lead to fractures. It can cause disability.

Imagine having so many spine fractures that you've lost inches in height and walk bent over. Imagine looking down at the ground everywhere you go because you can't straighten your back. Imagine not being able to find clothes that fit you. Imagine having difficulty breathing and eating because your lungs and stomach are compressed into a smaller space. Imagine having difficulty walking, let alone exercising, because of pain and misshapen bones. Imagine constantly having to be aware of what you are doing and having to do things so slowly and carefully because of a very real fear and dread of a fracture—a fracture that could lead to a drastic change in your life, including pain, loss of independence, loss of mobility, loss of freedom, and more.

Osteoporosis isn't just an "older person's" disease. Young women also experience fractures. Imagine being sidelined because of a broken bone and not being able to get those good feelings you get from regular activity.

EATING FOR HEALTHY BONES

How much calcium do I need? It's very important to your bone health that you receive adequate daily amounts of calcium, vitamin D, phosphorus, and magnesium. These vitamins and minerals are the most influential in building bones and teeth. This chart will help you decide how much calcium you need.

Recommended Calcium Intakes (mg/day)

Ages	Amount
9 to 13	1,300
14 to 18	1,300
19 to 30	1,000

Source: *National Academy of Sciences, 1997.*

Where can I get calcium and vitamin D? Dairy products are the primary food sources of calcium. Choose low-fat milk, yogurt, cheeses, ice cream, or products made or served with these choices to fulfill your daily requirement. Three servings of dairy products per day should give you at least 900 mg (milligrams) of calcium.

Green vegetables are another source. A cup of broccoli, for example, has about 136 mg of calcium. Sunlight is an important source of vitamin D, but when the sun isn't shining, turn to dietary sources of vitamin D.

Milk and dairy products. Many great snack and meal items contain calcium. With a little planning and "know-how," you can make meals and snacks calcium- rich!

Milk: Wouldn't a tall, cold glass of this refreshing thirst quencher be great right now? If you're concerned about fat and calories, choose reduced-fat or fat-free milk. You can drink it plain or with a low- or no-fat syrup or flavoring, such as chocolate syrup, vanilla extract, hazelnut flavoring, or cinnamon.

Cheese: Again, you can choose the low- or no-fat varieties. Use all different types of cheese for sandwiches, bagels, omelets, vegetable dishes, pasta creations, or as a snack by itself!

Pudding (prepared with milk): You can now purchase (or make from a mix) pudding in a variety of flavors with little or no fat, such as chocolate fudge, lemon, butterscotch, vanilla, and pistachio. Try them all!

Yogurt: Add fruit. Eat it plain. Add a low- or no-fat sauce or syrup. No matter how you choose to eat this calcium-rich food, yogurt remains a quick, easy, and convenient choice. It's also available in a variety of flavors. Try mocha-fudge-peppermint-swirl if you're more adventurous at heart and vanilla if you're a more traditional yogurt snacker!

Frozen yogurt (or fat-free ice cream): Everybody loves ice cream. And now, without the unnecessary fat, you can enjoy it more often! Mix yogurt, milk, and fruit to create a breakfast shake. Have a cone at lunchtime or as a snack. A scoop or two after dinner can be cool and refreshing.

What are other sources of calcium? Many foods you already buy and eat may be "calcium-fortified." Try calcium-fortified orange juice or calcium-fortified cereal. Check food labels to see if some of your other favorite foods may be good sources of calcium. You also can take calcium supplements if you think you may not be getting enough from your diet.

The National Institutes of Health Osteoporosis and Related Bone Diseases ~ National Resource Center acknowledges the assistance of the National Osteoporosis Foundation in the preparation of this publication.

Reviewed May 2009

In: Women in Sports
Editors: Amelia S. Halloway pp. 89-111

ISBN: 978-1-61728-161-7
© 2010 Nova Science Publishers, Inc.

Chapter 7

TITLE IX, SEX DISCRIMINATION, AND INTERCOLLEGIATE ATHLETICS: A LEGAL OVERVIEW

Jody Feder

SUMMARY

Enacted nearly four decades ago, Title IX of the Education Amendments of 1972 prohibits discrimination on the basis of sex in federally funded education programs or activities. Although the Title IX regulations bar recipients of federal financial assistance from discriminating on the basis of sex in a wide range of educational programs or activities, such as student admissions, scholarships, and access to courses, the statute is perhaps best known for prohibiting sex discrimination in intercollegiate athletics.

Indeed, the provisions regarding athletics have proved to be one of the more controversial aspects of Title IX. At the center of the debate is a three-part test that the Department of Education (ED) uses to determine whether institutions are providing nondiscriminatory athletic participation opportunities for both male and female students. Proponents of the existing regulations point to the dramatic increases in the number of female athletes in elementary and secondary school, college, and beyond as the ultimate indicator of the statute's success in breaking down barriers against women in sports. In contrast, opponents contend that the Title IX regulations unfairly impose quotas on collegiate sports and force universities to cut men's teams in order to remain in compliance. Critics further argue that the decline in certain men's sports, such as wrestling, is a direct result of Title IX's emphasis on proportionality in men's and women's college sports.

In 2002, ED appointed a commission to study Title IX and to recommend whether or not the athletics provisions should be revised. The Commission on Opportunity in Athletics delivered its final report to the Secretary of Education in 2003. In response, ED issued new guidance in 2003 and 2005 that clarified Title IX policy and the use of the three-part test.

This CRS report provides an overview of Title IX in general and the intercollegiate athletics regulations in particular, as well as a summary of the Commission's report and ED's response and a discussion of legal challenges to the regulations and to the three-part test. For related reports, see CRS Report RS22544, *Title IX and Single Sex Education: A Legal Analysis*, by Jody Feder.

In the 111th Congress, several bills related to Title IX have been introduced, including H.R. 2882, H.Res. 95, H.Res. 114, and S.Res. 55.

I. INTRODUCTION

Enacted nearly four decades ago, Title IX of the Education Amendments of 1972 prohibits discrimination on the basis of sex in federally funded education programs or activities.[1] Although the Title IX regulations bar recipients of federal financial assistance from discriminating on the basis of sex in a wide range of educational programs or activities, such as student admissions, scholarships, and access to courses, the statute is perhaps best known for prohibiting sex discrimination in intercollegiate athletics.

Indeed, the provisions regarding athletics have proved to be one of the more controversial aspects of Title IX. At the center of the debate is a three-part test that the Department of Education (ED) uses to determine whether institutions are providing nondiscriminatory athletic participation opportunities for both male and female students. Proponents of the existing regulations point to the dramatic increases in the number of female athletes in elementary and secondary school, college, and beyond as the ultimate indicator of the statute's success in breaking down barriers against women in sports. In contrast, critics contend that the Title IX regulations unfairly impose quotas on collegiate

---

[1] 20 U.S.C. §§ 1681 et seq.

sports and force universities to cut men's teams in order to remain in compliance.[2] Critics further argue that the decline in certain men's sports, such as wrestling, is a direct result of Title IX's emphasis on proportionality in men's and women's college sports.

In 2002, ED appointed a commission to study Title IX and to recommend whether or not the athletics provisions should be revised.[3] The Commission on Opportunity in Athletics delivered its final report to the Secretary of Education in 2003.[4] In response, ED issued new guidance in 2003 and 2005 that clarified Title IX policy and the use of the three-part test.[5]

This CRS report provides an overview of Title IX in general and the intercollegiate athletics regulations in particular, as well as a summary of the Commission's report and ED's response and a discussion of legal challenges to the regulations and to the three-part test. For related reports, see CRS Report RS22544, *Title IX and Single Sex Education: A Legal Analysis*, by Jody Feder.

In the 111th Congress, several bills related to Title IX have been introduced, including H.R. 2882, H.Res. 95, H.Res. 114, and S.Res. 55.

II. TITLE IX BACKGROUND

Enacted in response to a growing concern regarding disparities in the educational experiences of male and female students, Title IX is designed to eliminate sex discrimination in education. Although Title IX prohibits a broad range of discriminatory actions, such as sexual harassment in elementary and secondary schools or discrimination against women in graduate school admissions, Title IX is perhaps best known for its role in barring discrimination against women in college sports. Indeed, when the Department of Health, Education, and Welfare (HEW), which was the predecessor agency of the Department of Education, issued policy guidance regarding Title IX and

---

[2] June Kronholz, *College Coaches Press Bush on Title IX*, The Wall Street Journal, Aug. 27, 2002, at A4.

[3] Erik Brady, *Major Changes Debated for Title IX*, USA Today, Dec. 18, 2002, at A1.

[4] The Secretary of Education's Commission on Opportunity in Athletics, *"Open to All": Title IX at Thirty*, Feb. 28, 2003, http://www.ed.gov/about/bdscomm/list/athletics/report.html.

[5] Department of Education, Further Clarification of Intercollegiate Athletics Policy Guidance Regarding Title IX Compliance (July 11, 2003) (hereinafter 2003 Clarification); Department of Education, Additional Clarification on Intercollegiate Athletics Policy: Three-Part Test—Part Three (March 17, 2005) (hereinafter 2005 Clarification).

athletics, the agency specifically noted that participation rates for women in college sports "are far below those of men" and that "on most campuses, the primary problem confronting female athletes is the absence of a fair and adequate level of resources, services, and benefits."[6]

Federal law regarding Title IX intercollegiate athletics consists of three basic components: (1) the Title IX statute, which was enacted in the Education Amendments of 1972 and amended in the Education Amendments of 1974;[7] (2) the Department of Education regulations, which were originally issued in 1975 by HEW;[8] and (3) ED's policy guidance regarding Title IX athletics. The athletics policy guidance is primarily comprised of two documents: (1) a 1979 Policy Interpretation that established the controversial three-part test,[9] and (2) a 1996 Clarification of the three-part test, which reinvigorated enforcement of Title IX in intercollegiate athletics.[10] In addition, ED issued further clarifications in 2003 and 2005.[11] Despite the public attention generated by the three-part test, it is important to note that the test itself forms only a small part of the larger body of Title IX law. A general overview of the Title IX statute and regulations is provided below, while the athletics policy guidance and the legal debate surrounding Title IX and the three-part test are described in greater detail in subsequent sections.

In addition to this substantial body of Title IX law and policy, one other federal statute—the Equity in Athletics Disclosure Act[12]—also applies to intercollegiate athletics. Under this statute, colleges and universities are required to report statistical data, broken down by sex, on undergraduate enrollment and athletic participation and expenditures.

The Title IX Statute

Enacted nearly 40 years ago, the Title IX statute is designed to prevent sex

---

[6] Title IX of the Education Amendments of 1972; A Policy Interpretation: Title IX and Intercollegiate Athletics, 44 FR 71413, 71419 (Dec. 11, 1979) (hereinafter 1979 Policy Interpretation).

[7] P.L. 93-3 80.

[8] 34 CFR Part 106.

[9] 1979 Policy Interpretation, *supra* footnote 6, at 71413.

[10] Department of Education, Clarification of Intercollegiate Athletics Policy Guidance: The Three-Part Test (Jan. 16, 1996) (hereinafter 1996 Clarification).

[11] 2003 Clarification, *supra* footnote 5; 2005 Clarification, *supra* footnote 5.

[12] 20 U.S.C. § 1092(g).

discrimination by barring recipients of federal funds from discriminating in their education programs or activities. Specifically, the statute declares, "No person in the United States, shall, on the basis of sex, be excluded from participation in, be denied the benefits of, or be subjected to discrimination under any education program or activity receiving Federal financial assistance," subject to certain exceptions.[13]

The original Title IX legislation, which set forth the broad prohibition against sex discrimination but provided little detail about specific programs or activities, made no mention of college sports. However, the Education Amendments of 1974 directed HEW to issue Title IX implementing regulations "which shall include with respect to intercollegiate athletic activities reasonable provisions considering the nature of particular sports."[14] This provision was added after Congress eliminated a section that would have made revenue-producing sports exempt from Title IX.[15]

It is important to note that, under Title IX, the receipt of any amount of federal financial assistance is sufficient to trigger the broad nondiscrimination obligation embodied in the statute. This nondiscrimination obligation extends institution-wide to *all* education programs or activities operated by the recipient of the federal funds, even if some of the education programs or activities themselves are not funded with federal dollars.[16] For example, virtually all colleges and universities in the United States are recipients of federal financial assistance because they receive some form of federal aid, such as scientific research grants or student tuition financed by federal loans. Once a particular school is deemed a recipient of federal financial assistance, all of the education programs and activities that it operates are subject to Title IX. Thus, if a college or university receives federal assistance through its student financial aid program, its nondiscrimination obligation is not restricted solely to its student financial aid program, but rather the obligation extends to all of the education programs or activities conducted by the institution, including athletics and other programs that do not receive federal funds. The

---

[13] *Id.* at § 168 1(a). Exceptions include admissions to elementary and secondary schools, educational institutions of religious organizations with contrary religious tenets, military training institutions, educational institutions that are traditionally single-sex, fraternities and sororities, certain voluntary youth service organizations such as the Girl or Boy Scouts, father-son or mother-daughter activities at educational institutions, and beauty pageants. *Id.*

[14] P.L. 93-3 80 § 844.

[15] 1979 Policy Interpretation, *supra* footnote 6, at 71413.

[16] Department of Justice, Civil Rights Division, Title IX Legal Manual 51 (Jan. 11, 2001), *available at* http://www.usdoj.gov/crt/cor/coord/ixlegal.pdf.

provision regarding receipt of federal funds, therefore, is the primary mechanism for compelling institutions to comply with Title IX in their athletic programs.[17]

The Title IX Regulations

Because Title IX's prohibition against sex discrimination extends to all education programs or activities operated by recipients of federal funds, the scope of Title IX is quite broad. While the statute lays out only the general prohibition against sex discrimination, the implementing regulations specify the wide range of education programs or activities affected. Indeed, the regulations bar recipients from discriminating on the basis of sex in student admissions, recruitment, scholarship awards and tuition assistance, housing, access to courses and other academic offerings, counseling, financial assistance, employment assistance to students, health and insurance benefits and services, athletics, and all aspects of education-related employment, including recruitment, hiring, promotion, tenure, demotion, transfer, layoff, termination, compensation, benefits, job assignments and classifications, leave, and training.[18]

Despite the wide array of programs and activities subject to Title IX, it is the provisions on athletics that have generated the bulk of public attention and controversy in recent years. Under the Title IX regulations, recipients of federal financial assistance are prohibited from discriminating on the basis of sex in their sports programs. Specifically, the regulations declare, "No person shall, on the basis of sex, be excluded from participation in, be denied the benefits of, be treated differently from another person or otherwise be discriminated against in any interscholastic, intercollegiate, club or intramural

---

[17] For a brief period from 1984 to 1988, Title IX enforcement in college athletics was suspended as a result of a Supreme Court ruling that Title IX was "program-specific," meaning that the statute's requirements applied only to education programs that received federal funds and not to an institution's programs as a whole. Grove City College v. Bell, 465 U.S. 555, 574 (1984). Because few university athletic programs receive federal dollars, college sports were essentially exempt from Title IX coverage after this decision. In the Civil Rights Restoration Act of 1987 (P.L. 100- 259), however, Congress overrode the Supreme Court's interpretation of Title IX by passing legislation to clarify that Title IX's requirements apply institution-wide and are not program-specific, thus reinstating Title IX's coverage of athletics. 20 U.S.C. § 1687.

[18] 34 CFR §§ 106.31-106.56.

athletics offered by a recipient."[19] In addition, recipients are barred from providing athletics separately on the basis of sex, except under certain circumstances, such as when team selection is based on competitive skill or the activity is a contact sport.[20] Finally, the regulations require institutions that provide athletic scholarships to make such awards available in proportion to the numbers of male and female students participating in intercollegiate athletics.[21]

An important principle embodied in the Title IX regulations on athletics is the principle of equal opportunity. Under the regulations, recipients such as colleges and universities must "provide equal athletic opportunity for members of both sexes."[22] When evaluating whether equal opportunities are available, the Department of Education (ED) examines, among other factors, the provision of equipment and supplies, scheduling of games and practice time, travel and per diem allowance, opportunity to receive coaching and academic tutoring, assignment and compensation of coaches and tutors, provision of locker rooms and practice and competitive facilities, provision of medical training facilities and services, provision of housing and dining facilities and services, and publicity.[23] In addition, ED considers "whether the selection of sports and levels of competition effectively accommodate the interests and abilities of members of both sexes."[24] In order to measure compliance with this last factor, ED established the three-part test that has been challenged by opponents of existing Title IX policy.

To clarify how to comply with the intercollegiate athletics requirements contained in the Title IX regulations, ED issued a Policy Interpretation in 1979 and a subsequent Clarification of this guidance in 1996.[25] Combined, these two documents form the substantive basis of the policy guidance on the three-part test, which has generated the bulk of the questions and concerns surrounding Title IX and intercollegiate athletics. ED also issued a further clarification in 2003, but this document made only minor alterations to the 1979 Policy Interpretation and the 1996 Clarification.[26] In addition, in 2005,

---

[19] *Id.* at § 106.41(a).

[20] *Id.* at §106.41(b). Under the regulations, contact sports are defined to include boxing, wrestling, rugby, ice hockey, football, and basketball.

[21] *Id.* at § 106.3 7(c).

[22] *Id.* at § 106.41(c).

[23] *Id.*

[24] *Id.*

[25] 1979 Policy Interpretation, *supra* footnote 6; 1996 Clarification, *supra* footnote 10.

[26] 2003 Clarification, *supra* footnote 5.

ED issued yet another clarification that established a new way in which colleges may demonstrate compliance with the interest test prong of the three-part test.[27] These guidance documents are discussed in greater detail in the section below.

III. INTERCOLLEGIATE ATHLETICS AND THE POLICY GUIDANCE

As noted above, ED has set forth its interpretation of the intercollegiate athletics provisions of the Title IX statute and implementing regulations in two documents: the 1979 Policy Interpretation and the subsequent 1996 Clarification. These two documents, which remain in force, were designed to provide guidance to colleges and universities regarding how to achieve Title IX compliance by providing equal opportunity in their intercollegiate athletic programs. To that end, both of the guidance documents discuss the factors that ED considers when enforcing Title IX.[28]

Under the 1979 Policy Interpretation, HEW established three different standards to ensure equal opportunity in intercollegiate athletics.[29] First, with regard to athletic scholarships, the compliance standard is that such aid "should be available on a substantially proportional basis to the number of male and female participants in the institution's athletic program."[30] Second, HEW established a standard that male and female athletes should receive "equivalent treatment, benefits, and opportunities" in the following areas: equipment and supplies, games and practice times, travel and per diem, coaching and academic tutoring, assignment and compensation of coaches and tutors, locker rooms and practice and competitive facilities, medical and training facilities, housing and dining facilities, publicity, recruitment, and support services.[31] Finally, in terms of meeting the regulatory requirement to

---

[27] 2005 Clarification, *supra* footnote 5.

[28] 1979 Policy Interpretation, *supra* footnote 6; 1996 Clarification, *supra* footnote 10.

[29] Although the Policy Interpretation focuses on formal intercollegiate athletic programs, its requirements also apply to club, intramural, and interscholastic athletics. 1979 Policy Interpretation, *supra* footnote 6.

[30] *Id.* at 71414. This requirement, however, does not mean that schools must provide a proportional number of scholarships or that all individual scholarships must be of equal value; the only requirement is that the overall amount spent on scholarship aid must be proportional. *Id.* at 71415.

[31] *Id.* Such benefits, opportunities, and treatment need not be identical, and even a finding of nonequivalence can be justified by a showing of legitimate nondiscriminatory factors.

address the interests and abilities of male and female students alike, the compliance standard is that such interests and abilities must be equally effectively accommodated.[32]

In order to determine compliance with the latter accommodation standard, ED considers three additional factors: (1) the determination of athletic interests and abilities of students, (2) the selection of sports offered,[33] and (3) the levels of competition available, including the opportunity for team competition.[34] It is the criteria used to assess this third and final factor that form the basis of the three-part test. The three-part test, the debate over the test and its proportionality requirement, ED's Title IX review commission, and ED's response to the Commission's report are discussed in detail below.

The Three-Part Test

Under the Policy Interpretation, in accommodating the interests and abilities of athletes of both sexes, institutions must provide the opportunity for male and female athletes to participate in competitive sports. ED measures an institution's compliance with this requirement through one of the following three methods:

> (1) Whether intercollegiate level participation opportunities for male and female students are provided in numbers substantially proportionate to their respective enrollments; or (2) Where the members of one sex have been and are underrepresented among intercollegiate athletes, whether the institution can show a history and continuing practice of program expansion, which is demonstrably responsive to the developing interest and abilities of the members of that sex ; or (3) Where the members of one sex are underrepresented among intercollegiate athletes, and the institution cannot show a continuing practice of program expansion such as that cited above,

---

According to the Policy Interpretation, "some aspects of athletic programs may not be equivalent for men and women because of unique aspects of particular sports or athletic activities." The Policy Interpretation specifically cites football as an example of such a sport. *Id.*at 71415-16.

[32] *Id.* at 71414.

[33] According to the Policy Interpretation, "the regulation does not require institutions to integrate their teams nor to provide exactly the same choice of sports to men and women. However, where an institution sponsors a team in a particular sport for members of one sex, it may be required either to permit the excluded sex to try out for the team or to sponsor a separate team for the previously excluded sex." *Id.* at 71417-18.

[34] *Id.* at 71417.

whether it can be demonstrated that the interests and abilities of the members of that sex have been fully and effectively accommodated by the present program.[35]

These three methods for determining whether institutions are complying with the Title IX requirement to provide nondiscriminatory participation opportunities for both male and female athletes have come to be referred to as the three-part test. In its 1996 Clarification, which addresses only the three-part test, ED provides additional guidance for institutions seeking to comply with Title IX.

According to the 1996 Clarification, an institution must meet only one part of the three-part test in order to prove its compliance with the nondiscrimination requirement.[36] Thus, institutions may prove compliance by meeting (1) the proportionality test, which measures whether the ratio of male and female athletes is substantially proportional to the ratio of male and female students at the institution, (2) the expansion test, which measures whether an institution has a history and continuing practice of expanding athletic opportunities for the underrepresented sex, or (3) the interests test, which measures whether an institution is accommodating the athletic interests of the underrepresented sex.[37]

In addition, the 1996 Clarification reiterates that ED examines many other factors beyond those set forth in the three-part test when it evaluates an institution's Title IX athletics compliance.[38] The 1996 Clarification also provides a more detailed examination of the factors that ED considers under each of the three tests, as well as examples illustrating how the various factors affect a finding of compliance or noncompliance.[39]

The 2003 Clarification and the 2005 Clarification, which provide additional guidance regarding the three-part test, are discussed separately below.

---

[35] *Id.* at 71418.

[36] 1996 Clarification, *supra* footnote 10.

[37] Dear Colleague Letter from the Department of Education's Office for Civil Rights regarding the Clarification of Intercollegiate Athletics Policy Guidance: The Three-Part Test (Jan. 16, 1996), *available at* http://www.ed.gov/about/ offices/list/ocr/docs/clarific.html (hereinafter Dear Colleague Letter).

[38] 1996 Clarification, *supra* footnote 10.

[39] *Id.*

The Proportionality Test

The first prong of the three-part test—the proportionality test—is the most controversial. Indeed, critics contend that proportionality amounts to an unfair system of quotas. Because women's enrollment in postsecondary schools has increased dramatically in the decades since Title IX was enacted, rising 30% from 1981 to 1999,[40] critics argue that proportionality results in reverse discrimination, forcing schools to cut existing men's teams in order to create new slots for women.[41]

Proponents of proportionality respond that Title IX does not require quotas because schools that cannot demonstrate proportionality can still comply with Title IX if they pass one of the two remaining parts of the three-part test. Supporters also reject the notion that Title IX forces schools to eliminate men's teams, arguing that costly men's sports like football are to blame for cuts in less popular sports for both men and women. In addition, supporters note that instead of cutting men's sports, schools can achieve proportionality by adding women's teams.[42]

Critics counter that even though the three-part test offers an alternative to the proportionality approach in theory, in reality, maintaining proportionality is the only sure way to avoid a lawsuit. Furthermore, say critics, even though schools can technically comply with the proportionality standard by adding women's teams, budget realities often force institutions to cut men's teams instead. Proponents, however, respond that the vast majority of schools that add women's teams do not eliminate men's teams. Changing the proportionality test, say proponents, would be tantamount to repealing a law that is widely credited for dramatically increasing women's interest, participation, and success in sports.[43]

In 2001, the General Accounting Office (GAO) released a study of intercollegiate athletics. The GAO report included the following findings:

"The number of women participating in intercollegiate athletics at 4-year colleges and universities increased substantially—from 90,000 to 163,000— between school years 198 1-82 and 1998-99, while the

---

[40] General Accounting Office, Intercollegiate Athletics: Four-Year Colleges' Experiences Adding and Discontinuing Teams 8 (March 2001).

[41] Brady, *supra* footnote 3.

[42] *Id.*

[43] *Id.*

number of men participating increased more modestly—from 220,000 to 232,000."[44]

"Women's athletic participation grew at more than twice the rate of their growth in undergraduate enrollment, while men's participation more closely matched their growth in undergraduate enrollment."[45]

"The total number of women's teams increased from 5,595 to 9,479, a gain of 3,784 teams, compared to an increase from 9,113 to 9,149 teams for men, a gain of 36 teams."[46]

"Several women's sports and more than a dozen men's sports experienced net decreases in the number of teams. For women, the largest net decreases in the number of teams occurred in gymnastics; for men, the largest decreases were in wrestling."[47]

In men's sports, "the greatest increase in numbers of participants occurred in football, with about 7,200 more players. Football also had the greatest number of participants—approximately 60,000, or about twice as many as the next largest sport. Wrestling experienced the largest decrease in participation—a drop of more than 2,600 participants."[48]

"In all, 963 schools added teams and 307 discontinued teams since 1992-93. Most were able to add teams—usually women's teams—without discontinuing any teams."[49]

"Among the colleges and universities that added a women's team, the two factors cited most often as greatly influencing the decision were the need to address student interest in particular sports and the need to meet gender equity goals or requirements. Similarly, schools that discontinued a men's team cited a lack of student interest and gender equity concerns as the factors greatly influencing their decision, as well as the need to reallocate the athletic budget to other sports."[50]

---

[44] General Accounting Office, Intercollegiate Athletics: Four-Year Colleges' Experiences Adding and Discontinuing Teams 4 (March 2001).

[45] Id.

[46] Id.

[47] Id.

[48] Id. at 10.

[49] Id. at 5.

[50] Id.

ED's Interpretation of the Title IX Proportionality Test

Historically, ED has favored the proportionality approach to Title IX enforcement. Among the factors that ED considers under the proportionality test are the number of participation opportunities provided to athletes of both sexes. According to ED, "as a general rule, all athletes who are listed on a team's squad or eligibility list and are on the team as of the team's first competitive event are counted as participants."[51] ED next determines whether these participation opportunities are substantially proportionate to the ratio of male and female students enrolled at the institution, but, for reasons of flexibility, ED does not require exact proportionality.[52]

According to the 1996 Clarification, the proportionality test acts as a safe harbor. In other words, if an institution can demonstrate proportional athletic opportunities for women, then the institution will automatically be found to be in compliance.[53] If, however, an institution cannot prove proportionality, then the institution can still establish compliance by demonstrating that the imbalance does not reflect discrimination because the institution either (1) has a demonstrated history and continuing practice of expanding women's sports opportunities (prong two) or (2) has fully and effectively accommodated the athletic interests of women (prong three).

In its 2003 Clarification, ED specifically addressed the "safe harbor" language in the 1996 guidance. Noting that the "safe harbor" phrase had led many schools to believe erroneously that achieving compliance with Title IX could be guaranteed by meeting the proportionality test only, ED reiterated that "each of the three prongs of the test is an equally sufficient means of complying with Title IX, and no one prong is favored."[54]

Finally, the 1996 Clarification explicitly declares that "nothing in the three-part test requires an institution to eliminate participation opportunities for men" and challenges the notion that the three-part test requires quotas.[55] Rather, the 1996 Clarification states that "the three-part test gives institutions flexibility and control over their athletic programs."[56] Furthermore, the 1996 Clarification notes that the Policy Interpretation in general and the three-part

---

[51] 1996 Clarification, *supra* footnote 10.

[52] *Id.*

[53] Dear Colleague Letter, *supra* footnote 37.

[54] 2003 Clarification, *supra* footnote 5.

[55] 1996 Clarification, *supra* footnote 10.

[56] *Id.*

test in particular have been upheld by every court that has reviewed the guidance documents.[57]

The Title IX Review Commission

Although ED has enforced its Title IX policy, including the three-part test and its proportionality standard, virtually unchanged since shortly after the statute was enacted nearly four decades ago, several years ago the agency considered whether or not to alter its athletics policy. To that end, ED appointed the Commission on Opportunity in Athletics in June 2002 to review Title IX and to recommend changes if warranted. The commission, which held a series of meetings around the country to discuss problems with and improvements to Title IX, issued its final report containing findings and recommendations in February 2003.[58]

In its report, the Commission noted that it "found strong and broad support for the original intent of Title IX, coupled with a great deal of debate over how the law should be enforced," but that "more needs to be done to create opportunities for women and girls and retain opportunities for boys and men."[59] Ultimately, the final report contained 23 recommendations for strengthening Title IX, including 15 recommendations that were adopted unanimously. When the Commission issued its final report, however, two dissenting members of the panel refused to sign the document and instead issued a minority report in which they withdrew their support for two of the unanimous recommendations and raised concerns about several other unanimous recommendations.[60] The Secretary of Education indicated that he intended to consider changes only with respect to the unanimous recommendations of the Commission.

Among the unanimous recommendations of the Commission are suggestions that ED (1) reaffirm its commitment to eliminating discrimination; (2) clarify its guidance and promote consistency in enforcement; (3) avoid making changes to Title IX that undermine enforcement; (4) clarify that

---

[57] Dear Colleague Letter, *supra* footnote 37. For a brief review of significant Title IX court decisions, see the "Title IX and the Courts" section below.

[58] The Secretary of Education's Commission on Opportunity in Athletics, *"Open to All": Title IX at Thirty*, Feb. 28, 2003, http://www.ed.gov/about/bdscomm/list/athletics/report.html.

[59] *Id.* at 4, 21.

[60] Donna de Varona and Julie Foudy, *Minority Views on the Report of the Commission on Opportunity in Athletics*, Feb. 2003, http://www.nwlc.org/pdf/MinorityReportFeb26.pdf.

cutting teams in order to achieve compliance is a disfavored practice; (5) enforce Title IX aggressively by implementing sanctions against violators; (6) promote student interest in athletics at elementary and secondary schools; (7) support amendments to the Equity in Athletics Disclosure Act that would improve athletic reporting requirements; (8) disseminate information on the criteria it uses to help schools determine whether activities that they offer qualify as athletic opportunities; (9) encourage the National Collegiate Athletic Association to review its scholarship and other guidelines; (10) advise schools that walk-on opportunities are not limited for schools that comply with the second or third prong of the three-part test; (11) examine the prospect of allowing institutions to demonstrate compliance with the third prong of the three-part test by comparing the ratio of male and female athletic participation with the demonstrated interests and abilities shown by regional, state, or national youth or high school participation rates or by interest levels indicated in student surveys; (12) abandon the "safe harbor" designation for the proportionality test in favor of treating each of the three tests equally; and (13) consider revising the second prong of the three-part test, possibly by designating a point at which a school can no longer establish compliance through this part.[61]

The Commission originally adopted an additional two recommendations unanimously, but the two dissenting members of the panel withdrew their support for these recommendations upon further opportunity for review of the final report. These contested recommendations suggest that ED (1) clarify the meaning of "substantial proportionality" to allow for a reasonable variance in the ratio of men's and women's athletic participation; and (2) explore additional ways of demonstrating equity beyond the three-part test.[62]

Other recommendations that the Commission adopted by a majority, but not unanimous, vote included suggestions that ED (1) adopt any future changes to Title IX through the normal federal rulemaking process; (2) encourage the reduction of excessive expenditures in intercollegiate athletics, possibly by exploring an antitrust exemption for college sports; (3) inform universities about the current requirements governing private funding of certain sports; (4) reexamine its requirements governing private funding of certain sports to allow such funding of sports that would otherwise be cut; (5)

---

[61] The Secretary of Education's Commission on Opportunity in Athletics, *"Open to All": Title IX at Thirty*, Feb. 28, 2003, 33-40, *http://www.ed.gov/about/bdscomm/list/* athletics/ report.html.

[62] Donna de Varona and Julie Foudy, *Minority Views on the Report of the Commission on Opportunity in Athletics*, Feb. 2003, http://www.nwlc.org/pdf/MinorityReportFeb26.pdf.

allow schools to comply with the proportionality test by counting the available slots on sports teams rather than actual participants; (6) for purposes of the proportionality test, exclude from the participation count walk-on athletes, who are non- scholarship players that tend to be male; (7) allow schools to conduct interest surveys to demonstrate compliance with the three-part test; and (8) for purposes of the proportionality test, exclude nontraditional students, who tend to be female, from the count of enrolled students. In addition, the Commission was evenly divided on a recommendation that would allow schools to meet the proportionality test if athletic participation rates were 50% male and 50% female, with a variance of two to three percentage points allowed.[63]

ED's Response to the Title IX Commission: The 2003 and 2005 Clarifications

In response to the Commission's report, ED indicated that it would study the recommendations and consider whether or not to revise its Title IX athletics policy.[64] Several months later, ED issued new guidance that essentially left the existing Title IX policy unchanged. In its 2003 Clarification, which provided further guidance regarding Title IX policy and the three-part test, ED reiterated that all three prongs of the three-part test have been and can be used to demonstrate compliance with Title IX, and the agency encouraged schools to use the approach that best suits its needs. In addition, the 2003 Clarification declared that complying with Title IX does not require schools to cut teams and that eliminating teams is a disfavored practice. The 2003 Clarification also noted that ED expects both to provide technical assistance to schools and to aggressively enforce Title IX. Finally, the guidance indicated that ED will continue to allow private sponsorship of athletic teams.[65]

In 2005, ED issued yet another clarification of the three-part test.[66] In the 2005 Clarification, ED provided additional guidance with respect to part three

---

[63] The Secretary of Education's Commission on Opportunity in Athletics, *"Open to All": Title IX at Thirty*, Feb. 28, 2003, 33-40, http://www.ed.gov/about/bdscomm/list/athletics/report.html.

[64] ED also recently amended the Title IX regulations in order to encourage single-sex classes and schools. 71 FR 62530.

[65] 2003 Clarification, *supra* footnote 5.

[66] 2005 Clarification, *supra* footnote 5.

of the three-part test. Under that test, known as the interests test, an institution may demonstrate compliance with Title IX by establishing that it is accommodating the athletic interests of the underrepresented sex. The new guidance clarified that one of the ways in which schools may demonstrate compliance with the interests test is by using an online survey to establish that the underrepresented sex has no unmet interests in athletic participation. Such a survey must be administered periodically to all students that are members of the underrepresented sex, and students must be informed that a failure to respond to the survey will be viewed as an indication of a lack of interest. As a result, the survey must be administered in a way designed to generate high response rates.

The 2005 Clarification emphasized that schools have flexibility to demonstrate compliance under any one part of the three-part test and that schools who choose to demonstrate compliance through the interests test have the option to do so in several ways. Among the factors that ED considers when determining whether the school has accurately measured student interest are surveys, requests for the addition of a varsity team, participation in club or intramural sports, participation rates in local high schools and athletic organizations, and intercollegiate participation rates in the school's region. Even if a school's population of the underrepresented sex is found to have an unmet interest in sports, the institution will not be found to have violated Title IX unless ED also finds that there is sufficient ability to sustain a team and a reasonable expectation of intercollegiate competition in the sport within the school's normal competitive region.[67]

IV. TITLE IX AND THE COURTS

Over the years, the Supreme Court has heard several cases pertaining to Title IX. Until a recent decision in 2005, none of these cases involved college or high school sports, but they did help to shape the legal landscape surrounding Title IX athletics policy. For example, in 1979, the Supreme Court held that Title IX includes a private right of action.[68] This decision strengthened Title IX enforcement because it means that an individual can sue in court for violations under the statute rather than wait for ED to pursue a complaint administratively. The Court further strengthened Title IX

---

[67] Id.

[68] Cannon v. Univ. of Chicago, 441 U.S. 677 (1979).

enforcement in 1992, when it ruled that individuals could sue for money damages in a Title IX lawsuit.[69] Finally, in a decision that was later overturned by Congress, the Court ruled that Title IX did not apply to an entire educational institution but rather applied only to the portion of the institution that received federal funds.[70]

In 2005, the Court handed down its decision in *Jackson v. Birmingham Board of Education.*[71] In this case, which involved a girl's basketball coach who claimed that he was removed from his coaching position in retaliation for his complaints about unequal treatment of the girl's team, the Court held that Title IX not only encompasses retaliation claims, but also is available to individuals who complain about sex discrimination, even if such individuals themselves are not the direct victims of sex discrimination.[72] Reasoning that "Title IX's enforcement scheme would unravel" "if retaliation went unpunished,"[73] the Court concluded that "when a funding recipient retaliates against a person because he complains of sex discrimination, this constitutes intentional discrimination on the basis of sex in violation of Title IX.[74]

Although the Supreme Court has decided only one case that directly involves Title IX athletics, the lower federal courts have heard multiple challenges to the statute and regulations. In fact, all of the federal courts of appeals that have considered the athletics Policy Interpretation, the three- part test, and the proportionality rule have upheld ED's Title IX regulations and policy.[75] In general, these courts have noted that the regulations and guidance represent a reasonable agency interpretation of Title IX, and they have ruled that the three-part test does not unfairly impose quotas because institutions

---

[69] Franklin v. Gwinnett County Public Schools, 503 U.S. 60 (1992).

[70] Grove City College v. Bell, 465 U.S. 555 (1984). *See also supra* notes 16-17 and accompanying text.

[71] 125 S.Ct. 1497 (2005).

[72] *Id.* at 1502.

[73] *Id.* at 1508.

[74] *Id.* at 1504 [internal quotations omitted].

[75] *See, e.g.,* Chalenor v. Univ. of North Dakota, 291 F.3d 1042 (8th Cir. 2002); Pederson v. Louisiana State Univ., 213 F.3d 858 (5th Cir. 2000); Neal v. Bd. of Trustees, 198 F.3d 763 (9th Cir. 1999); Horner v. Kentucky High Sch. Athletic Ass'n, 43 F.3d 265 (6th Cir. 1994); Kelley v. Bd. of Trustees, 35 F.3d 265(7th Cir. 1994), *cert. denied,* 513 U.S. 1128; Williams v. Sch. Dist. of Bethlehem, 998 F.2d 168 (3d Cir. 1993); Roberts v. Colorado State Bd. of Agric., 998 F.2d 824 (10th Cir. 1993), *cert. denied,* 510 U.S. 1004; Cohen v. Brown Univ., 991 F.2d 888 (1st Cir. 1993) (hereinafter Cohen I). In addition, in a second appeal on a separate issue in the *Cohen* case, the First Circuit strongly reiterated its previous ruling upholding Title IX. Cohen v. Brown Univ., 101 F.3d 155 (1st Cir. 1996), *cert. denied,* 520 U.S. 1186 (hereinafter Cohen II).

may select from two other methods besides proportionality in order to comply with Title IX. Indeed, in 1993, the First Circuit reached this conclusion in *Cohen v. Brown University*, a landmark Title IX case that was the first federal appeals court decision regarding Title IX athletics.[76] This section provides a brief summary of the *Cohen* decision, as well as a description of the National Wrestling Coaches Association lawsuit, which has been dismissed, and more recent cases involving the question of whether high school sports associations discriminate when they schedule boys and girls' sports in different seasons.

Cohen v. Brown University

In the *Cohen* case, female athletes at Brown University sued under Title IX when the school eliminated two women's sports—gymnastics and volleyball—and two male teams—golf and water polo—in a cost-cutting measure.[77] Although the cuts made far larger reductions in the women's athletic budget than in the men's, the cuts did not affect the ratio of male to female athletes, which remained roughly 63% male to 37% female, despite a student body that was approximately 52% male and 48% female.[78] In their lawsuit, the members of the women's gymnastics and volleyball teams "charged that Brown's athletic arrangements violated Title IX's ban on gender-based discrimination."[79] When the district court ordered the university to reinstate the two women's teams pending a full trial on the merits, Brown appealed by challenging the validity of both the Title IX guidance in general and the three-part test in particular. The First Circuit, however, affirmed the district court's decision in favor of the female athletes.[80]

In reaching its decision to uphold the validity of the three-part test, the First Circuit emphasized that ED's interpretation of Title IX warranted deference. According to the court, "the degree of deference is particularly high in Title IX cases because Congress explicitly delegated to the agency the task of prescribing standards for athletic programs under Title IX."[81] Thus, the court adopted ED's three-part test as an acceptable standard by which to

---

[76] 991 F.2d 888, 891 (1st Cir. 1993).

[77] *Id.* at 892.

[78] *Id.*

[79] *Id* at 893.

[80] *Id.* at 891.

[81] *Id.* at 895.

measure an institution's compliance with Title IX, as have all other appeals courts to subsequently consider the issue.[82]

Next, the court in *Cohen* turned to the question of whether the university had met any one part of the three-part test. Because there was a large disparity between the proportion of women at Brown who were students versus the proportion who were athletes and because the university had not demonstrated a history of expanding women's sports, the court focused its inquiry on whether or not Brown had met part three of the test by effectively accommodating student interest. The university argued that when measuring interest under this standard, the relative athletic interests of male and female students should be the proper point of comparison rather than the relative enrollment of male and female students.[83] In effect, Brown argued that its female students were less interested in sports than its male students and that its Title IX compliance should thus be measured by this standard.

Under ED's construction of the accommodation test, however, institutions must ensure participation opportunities where there is "sufficient interest and ability among the members of the excluded sex to sustain a viable team and a reasonable expectation of intercollegiate competition for that team."[84] Noting that this standard does not require institutions to provide additional athletic opportunities every time female students express interest, the court upheld the district court's finding that the existence and success of women's gymnastics and volleyball at Brown demonstrated that there was sufficient interest in and expectation of competition in those sports to rule in favor of the female athletes with regard to the third prong of the three-part test.[85] In a subsequent appeal in the *Cohen* case, the court explicitly noted that Brown's view of the accommodation test, which seems to assume that women are naturally less

---

[82] *See, e.g.*, Chalenor v. Univ. of North Dakota, 291 F.3d 1042 (8th Cir. 2002); Pederson v. Louisiana State Univ., 213 F.3d 858 (5th Cir. 2000); Neal v. Bd. of Trustees, 198 F.3d 763 (9th Cir. 1999); Horner v. Kentucky High Sch. Athletic Ass'n, 43 F.3d 265 (6th Cir. 1994); Kelley v. Bd. of Trustees, 35 F.3d 265(7th Cir. 1994), *cert. denied*, 513 U.S. 1128; Williams v. Sch. Dist. of Bethlehem, 998 F.2d 168 (3d Cir. 1993); Roberts v. Colorado State Bd. of Agric., 998 F.2d 824 (10th Cir. 1993), *cert. denied*, 510 U.S. 1004; Cohen v. Brown Univ., 991 F.2d 888 (1st Cir. 1993) (Cohen I). In addition, in a second appeal on a separate issue in the *Cohen* case, the First Circuit strongly reiterated its previous ruling upholding Title IX. Cohen v. Brown Univ., 101 F.3d 155 (1st Cir. 1996), *cert. denied*, 520 U.S. 1186 (Cohen II).

[83] Cohen I, 991 F.2d at 899.

[84] 1979 Policy Interpretation, *supra* footnote 6, at 71418.

[85] Cohen I, 991 F.2d at 904.

interested in sports than men, reflects invidious gender stereotypes and could potentially freeze in place any existing disparity in athletic participation.[86]

Finally, the court rejected the university's constitutional challenge, ruling that Title IX does not violate the Equal Protection clause of the Fourteenth Amendment.[87] In a subsequent appeal in the *Cohen* case, the court emphasized this point:

> No aspect of the Title IX regime at issue in this case – inclusive of the statute, the relevant regulation, and the pertinent agency documents – mandates gender-based preferences or quotas, or specific timetables for implementing numerical goals.... Race- and gender- conscious remedies are both appropriate and constitutionally permissible under a federal anti-discrimination regime, although such remedial measures are still subject to equal protection review.[88]

Challenges to Sports Scheduling Decisions

More recently, some parents and students have begun filing lawsuits that challenge the decision of certain state high school sports associations to schedule girls' sports in nontraditional seasons that differ from the season for corresponding boys' sports, arguing that the scheduling disparity violates the Equal Protection clause of the Constitution and Title IX. In Michigan, for example, a federal district court ruled that the Michigan High School Athletic Association's (MHSAA) scheduling of high school sports seasons in Michigan discriminated against female athletes on the basis of gender and thus violated the Constitution and Title IX.[89] Without reaching the statutory Title IX argument, the U.S. Court of Appeals for the Sixth Circuit upheld the district court on constitutional grounds.[90] Although this type of Title IX lawsuit

---

[86] Cohen II, 101 F.3d 155, 176.

[87] Cohen I, 991 F.2d at 900-01.

[88] Cohen II, 101 F.3d at 170, 172.

[89] Cmtys. for Equity v. Michigan High Sch. Athletic Ass'n., 178 F. Supp. 2d 805 (W.D.Mich.2001).

[90] Cmtys. for Equity v. Mich. High School Athletic Ass'n, 377 F. 3d 504 (6th Cir. 2004). The Supreme Court vacated and remanded the Sixth Circuit decision, Mich. High School Athletic Ass'n v. Cmtys. for Equity, 544 U.S. 1012 (2005), but the Sixth Circuit upheld its decision on remand. Cmtys. for Equity v. Mich. High School Athletic Ass'n, 459 F.3d 676 (6th Cir. 2006), cert. denied, Mich. High Sch. Ath. Ass'n v. Cmtys. for Equity, 127 S. Ct. 1912 (2007).

appears to have emerged only in recent years, similar legal challenges have occurred in other states.[91]

The National Wrestling Coaches Association Lawsuit

Meanwhile, disturbed by the decline in the number of men's wrestling teams at colleges and universities across the country, the National Wrestling Coaches Association (NWCA), together with former wrestling teams at several institutions, filed a lawsuit against ED in 2002, arguing that the Title IX regulations were adopted illegally and that Title IX unfairly discriminates against men.[92] In the lawsuit, the NWCA argued (1) that ED's establishment of the Title IX regulations and policy guidance was procedurally defective, (2) that ED exceeded its authority under the Title IX statute when enacting those regulations and guidance, and (3) that ED's regulations and guidance discriminate against male athletes, thereby violating the Title IX statute and the Equal Protection clause of the Fourteenth Amendment.[93]

In response to the lawsuit, ED, backed by the Bush Administration, moved to dismiss the case on the grounds that (1) the plaintiffs lacked standing to bring the case; (2) judicial review was unauthorized under the circumstances of this particular case; and (3) the suit was barred by the statute of limitations.[94] The National Women's Law Center (NWLC) filed an amicus brief in support of ED, arguing that the suit was improper because there was no guarantee that institutions would reinstate men's sports teams even if the Title IX regulations and policy were changed. The NWLC further observed that arguments similar to those made in the NWCA lawsuit had been rejected by every federal appeals court to consider the issue of Title IX.[95] Ultimately, the NWCA lawsuit was dismissed from federal court on the grounds that the

---

[91] *Review is Sought on Girls' Sports Ruling*, Wash. Post, May 3, 2005, at D02.

[92] Lori Nickel and Nahal Toosi, *Title IX is Taken To Task*, Milwaukee Journal Sentinel, Jan. 17, 2002 at C1.

[93] Complaint for Declaratory and Injunctive Relief, Nat'l Wrestling Coaches Ass'n v. Dep't of Educ., Civil Action No. 1 :02CV00072-EGS, available at http://www.nwcaonline.com.

[94] Defendant's Motion to Dismiss, Nat'l Wrestling Coaches Ass'n v. Dep't of Educ., Civil Action No. 1 :02CV00072- EGS, available at http://www.ed.gov/news/pressreleases/2002/05/wrestling.dismiss.mem.fin.pdf.

[95] Brief of Amici Curiae, Nat'l Wrestling Coaches Ass'n v. Dep't of Educ., Civil action No. 1 :02CV00072-EGS, available at http://www.nwlc.org/pdf/amicusbrief.final.pdf.

plaintiffs lacked the proper standing to bring the case.[96] The dismissal was affirmed by an appeals court,[97] and the Supreme Court effectively upheld the dismissal when it refused to review the case.[98]

Given the results in the NWCA case and in other Title IX cases brought before the federal courts of appeals, it seems likely that the courts will continue to defer to ED with regard to Title IX athletics policy in the near future. As noted above, ED has indicated that it intends to continue to use the three-part test to enforce Title IX. However, Congress could, if it disapproves of ED's Title IX athletics policy, respond with legislation to override the current regulations and guidance.

---

[96] Nat'l Wrestling Coaches Ass'n v. Dep't of Educ., 263 F. Supp. 2d 82, at 129-30 (D.D.C. June 11, 2003).

[97] Nat'l Wrestling Coaches Ass'n v. Dep't of Educ., 361 U.S. App. D.C. 257 (D.C. Cir. May 14, 2004).

[98] Nat'l Wrestling Coaches Ass'n v. Dep't of Educ., 545 U.S. 1104 (U.S. 2005).

In: Women in Sports pp. 113-120
Editors: Amelia S. Halloway

ISBN: 978-1-61728-161-7
© 2010 Nova Science Publishers, Inc.

Chapter 8

STATEMENT OF DOMINIQUE DAWES, PRESIDENT OF THE WOMEN'S SPORTS FOUNDATION, BEFORE THE COMMITTEE ON COMMERCE, SCIENCE AND TRANSPORTATION, U.S. SENATE

Dominique Dawes

I am Dominique Dawes, president of the Women's Sports Foundation, a 501 (c) (3) nonprofit national educational organization. The Foundation was founded in 1974 by Billie Jean King, to advance the lives of girls and women through sports and physical activity. Billie Jean and a host of legendary athletes leaders who like me, have served as President of the Foundation, did not want girls following in their footsteps to face the same barriers to participation as they did. To address the needs of girls and women in sports, the Foundation produces programming in four areas: education, advocacy, recognition and grants and is among the top ten public women's grant-giving funds in the nation.

As an athlete, I have had the privilege of representing the United States in three Olympic Games: 2000, 1996, 1992 and was a member of the 1996 Olympic women's team that clinched the first-ever gymnastics team gold medal for the United States. In addition to the team gold medal, I won an individual bronze medal in the floor exercise at the 1996 Olympic Games, becoming the first African-American to win an individual event medal in gymnastics. On Aug. 13, 2005 I was honored to be inducted into the USA Gymnastics Hall of Fame. I am also a television sports commentary and analyst and I coach gymnastics privately at Hill's Gymnastics in Gaithersburg, Md., the gym where I grew up training. I am also a spokesperson for the Girls Scouts "uniquely ME" program which builds girls' self esteem and empowers them to fulfill their potential. I am a graduate of the University of Maryland, College Park, with a degree in communications.

Today is National Girls and Women in Sports Day and I am also here representing the seven co-sponsoring agencies of the Day: the American Association of University Women (AAUW), Girls Incorporated, Girl Scouts of U.S.A., the National Association for Girls and Women in Sport (NAGWS), National Women's Law Center (NWLC), the Women's Sports Foundation (WSF), and the YWCA of the U.S.A. (YWCA).

I am here before you to express concern about the current state of inactivity among girls and how non-compliance with Title IX, the lack of equal opportunity in schools and colleges and open amateur sports and our current media culture contributes to girls being at higher risk for chronic diseases that are the result of sedentary lifestyles. While others on this panel will address the issue of inequity of sports opportunities, I would like to place in perspective what is at stake if we do not equally encourage our sons and daughters to participate in sports and engage in regular physical activity.

GIRLS AT HIGHER RISK FOR PHYSICAL INACTIVITY

The current widespread American support for equal treatment of males and females in sports is directly related to the fact that the public now understands that sports and physical activity are essential for the health and well-being of our children. We are in the midst of an obesity epidemic that has been created by sedentary lifestyles and poor nutrition habits. If we do nothing to change these circumstances, one in three children born in the year 2000 will develop Type II diabetes[1].

We also know that girls are at greater risk for inactivity in our society than boys, especially girls from underserved and lower socioeconomic populations. By the time a girl is 17 years old she has seen 250,000 television commercials

---

[1] Journal of the American Medical Association. (2003). 290:1884-1890.

focusing on her looks – not her health or physical abilities.[2] Forty-two percent of girls in grades one through three want to be thinner[3], 51% of 9-10 year old girls feel better about themselves when dieting[4] and 53% of 13 year old girls are unhappy with their bodies, increasing to 78% at age 17[5]. The media has convinced girls that "big" is unattractive and they must achieve an unattainable body type, even though big girls can be fit and healthy. One in six girls is now obese or overweight contrasted to one in 21 in 1970[6]. Black girls are twice as likely to be overweight as white girls.[7] If a girl does not participate in sports by the time she is 10 years old, there is only a 10% chance she will participate when she reaches the age of 25.[8] Between middle school and high school, girls drop out of sport at a rate that is double that of boys.[9] By the age of 16 or 17 only one in seven girls attends physical education class daily and 15-30% report no regular physical activity at all.[10] High school boys receive 40% more chances to play varsity sports than girls with similar statistics in college.[11]

---

[2] Mediascope. (2003). Body Image and Advertising. Online.   Retrieved   from   *http://www.* mediascope. org/pubs/ibriefs/bia.htm.

[3] Colton, M. and Core, S. (1991). Risk, Resiliency, and Resistance: Current Research on Adolescent Girls. Ms. Foundation.

[4] McNutt, S., Hu, Y., Schreiber, G.B., Crawford, P., Obarzanek, E., and Mellin, L., (1999). "A longitudinal study of dietary practices of black and white girls 9 and 10 years old at enrollment: The NHLBI growth and health study." Journal of Adolescent Health, 20(1):27-37.

[5] Brumberg J. (1998). The Body Project: An Intimate History of American Girls. NY: Vintage.

[6] National Center for Health Statistics. (2002). Health, United States, 2002. Hyattsville, MD, 2002.

[7] Centers for Disease Control and Prevention. (1999-2000).   National Health and Nutrition Examination Survey, 1999-2000.

[8] Linda Bunker, University of Virginia. (1988). Lifelong Benefits of Sports Participation for Girls and Women, Presented at the Sport Psychology Conference, University of Virginia, Charlottesville, June 22.

[9] U.S. Secretary of Health and Human Services and U.S. Secretary of Education. (2000)

[10] Centers for Disease Control and Prevention. (2002). "Surveillance Summaries." Morbidity and Mortality Weekly Report, 51 (No.SS-4).

[11] National Federation of State High School Associations. (2003). NFHS Handbook 2003-3004. Indianapolis, IN: National Federation of State High School Associations.; National Collegiate Athletic Association. Participation Statistics.2001 -2002. Can be retrieved at www.ncaa.org.

SPORT AND PHYSICAL ACTIVITY: AN EFFECTIVE INTERVENTION

We know that sport and physical activity are effective interventions to addressing the obesity crisis and research shows that sports and physical activity participation has an incredibly positive impact on the lives of girls and women. A 2004 compilation of research on the relationship of girls' and women's health by the Women's Sports Foundation summarized these benefits.[12] Regular participation in physical activity during childhood and adolescence promotes the development of positive body image[13], confidence[14], and self-esteem[15]. Girls who participate in sports and physical activity are academically more successful[16], more likely to graduate from high school[17], more likely to matriculate in college[18], and experience greater career success[19]. Participation in sports and other physical activities can help reduce a girl's health risk for obesity[20], diabetes[21], heart disease[22], osteoporosis[23], breast

---

[12] Sabo, D., Miller, K. E., Melnick, M. J. & Heywood, L. (2004). Her Life Depends On It: Sport, Physical Activity, and the Health and Well-Being of American Girls. East Meadow, NY: Women's Sports Foundation.

[13] Women's Sports Foundation, 2001; President's Council on Physical Fitness and Sports, 1997; Colton, M., and Gore, S. (1991). Risk, Resiliency, and Resistance: Current Research on Adolescent Girls. Ms.Foundation.; Women's Sports Foundation, 1985).

[14] President's Council on Physical Fitness and Sport. (1997) Physical Activity & Sport in the Lives of Girls; Women's SportsMiller Lite Report, 1985; Melpomene Institute, 1995)

[15] Fox, 1988, 2000; Guinn, Semper and Jorgensen, 1997; Palmer, 1995; Sonstroem,1984, 1997).

[16] Sabo, D., Melnick, M., and Vanfossen, B. (1989) The Women's Sports Foundation Report: Minorities in Sports. New York: Women's Sports Foundation, Eisenhower Park, East Meadow, NY 11554.

[17] Sabo, D., Melnick, M., and Vanfossen, B. (1989) The Women's Sports Foundation Report: Minorities in Sports. New York: Women's Sports Foundation, Eisenhower Park, East Meadow, NY 11554.

[18] Marsh, H.W. and Kleitman, S. (2003). "School athletic participation: Mostly gain with little pain." Journal of Sport and Exercise Psychology, 25: 205-228.

[19] Bunker, L.K. "Life-long Benefits of Youth Sport Participation for Girls and Women." Presented at the Sport Psychology Conference, University of Virginia, Charlottesville, June 22, 1988, Game Face, From the Locker Room to the Boardroom: A Survey on Sports in the Lives of Women Business Executives, Feb. 2002

[20] U.S. Department of Health and Human Services. (1996), Physical Activity and Health: a Report of the Surgeon General. Atlanta, GA: U.S. Department of Health and Human Resources, Centers for Disease Control and Prevention, National Center for Chronic Disease Prevention and Health Promotion. Colditz, G.A. (1999).; "Economic costs of obesity and inactivity. (Physical Activity in the Prevention and Treatment of Obesity and its Comorbidities)" Medicine and Science in Sports and Exercise, 31: 5663-68.; Ward, D., Trost, S., Felton, G., Saunders, R., Parsons, M., Dowda, M., and Pate, R. (1997). "Physical

cancer[24], depression[25], unintended teen pregnancy[26], anxiety and lack of self-esteem[27] among others.

activity and physical fitness in African-American girls with and without obesity." Obesity Research, 5: 572-577.

[21] Associated Press (2003). "Diabetes in children set to soar." MSNBC. June 16, 2003. Colditz, G.A. (1999). "Economic costs of obesity and inactivity. (Physical Activity in the Prevention and Treatment of Obesity and its Comorbidities)" Medicine and Science in Sports and Exercise, 31: 5663-68.

[22] Centers for Disease Control and Prevention Center. (1995) National Health and Nutrition Examination Survey III 1994.; National Center for Chronic Disease Prevention and Health Promotion. (1996). Physical Activity and Health, A Report of the Surgeon General, (S/N 01 7-023- 00196-5). Washington, DC: U.S. Department of Health and Human Services.; Haddock, B.L., et al., (1998). "Cardiorespiratory fitness and cardiovascular disease risk factors in postmenopausal women." Medical Science and Sport Exercise, 30:893-898.; Kendig, S., and Sanford, D. (1998). Midlife and menopause: Celebrating women's health. AWHONN Symposia Series. Washington, DC: AWHONN.

[23] Kannus, P. (1999). "Preventing osteoporosis, falls, and fractures among elderly people." British Medical Journal, 318:205-206.; Teegarden et al, (1996). "Previous physical activity relates to bone mineral measures in young women." Medicine and Science in Sports and Exercise, 28(1:105-113).; Bonaiuti, D., et al. (2002). "Exercise for preventing and treating osteoporosis in postmenopausal women (Cochrane Review)." In The Cochrane Library, Issue 3, Update Software.

[24] Bernstein, L., Henderson, B., Hanisch, R., Sullivan-Halley, J., and Ross, R. (1994). "Physical Exercise and reduced risk of breast cancer in young women." Journal of the National Cancer Institute, Vol. 86: 1403-1408.; Thune, I., et al. (1997). "Physical activity and the risk of breast cancer." New England Journal of Medicine, 18:1269-1275.; McTiernan, et al. (2003). "Recreational physical activity and the risk of breast cancer in postmenopausal women: The Women's Health Initiative Cohort Study." Journal of the American Medical Association, September 10; 290®10): 1331-6.; Patel, et al. (2003). "Recreational physical activity and risk of postmenopausal breast concern in a large cohort of US women." Cancer Causes Control, (6):519-529.

[25] Dunn, A.L., Trivedi, M.H., and O'Neal, H.A. (2001). "Physical activity dose-response effects on outcomes of depression and anxiety." Medicine and Science in Sports and Exercise, 33 (6):S587- S597.; Dimeo, F., Bauer, M., Varahram, I., Proest, G., and Halter, U. (2001). "Benefits from aerobic exercise in patients with major depression: a pilot study." British Journal of Sports Medicine, 35: 114-117.; Page, R.M., and Tucker, R.A. (1994). "Psychosocial discomfort and exercise frequency: An epidemiological study of adolescents." Adolescence, 29®1 1 3)"1 83-101.; Nicoloff, G.,and Schwenk, T.S. (1995). "Using exercise to ward off depression." Physician and Sportsmedicine, 23(9):44-58.; Ahmadi, J. et al, (2002). "Various Types of exercise and scores on the Beck Depression Inventory." Psychological Reports, 90(3)821-822.; Sanders, C.E. et al, (2000)."Moderate involvement in sports is related to lower depression levels in adolescents." Adolescence, 35(1 40):793-797.

[26] Dodge, T., and Jaccard, J. (2002). "Participation in athletics and female sexual risk behavior: The evaluation of four causal structures." Journal of Adolescent Research, 17:42-67.; Miller, K.E. et al, (1999). "Sports, sexual activity, contraceptive use, and pregnancy among female and male high school students: Testing cultural resource theory." Sociology of Sport Journal, 16:366-387.; Page, R.M. et al, (1998). "Is school sports participation a protective factor against adolescent health risk behaviors?" Journal of Health Education, 29(3):186-

A physical activity intervention is essential if we want to change the following startling statistics:

1 in every 6 girls is obese or overweight[28]; and as women, are 60% more likely to die from breast cancer[29]

1 in 3 teens get pregnant by the age of 20[30]

1 in 3 girls in grades 9-12 currently smoke[31]; lung cancer is the leading cause of cancer deaths among women[32]

1 in 3 adolescent girls will experience depression[33], anxiety or eating disorders[34]

Girls aged 4-19 have significantly higher "bad" cholesterol levels than boys; heart disease is the #1 cause of death among American women[35]

192.; Rome,E.S., Rybicki, L.A., and Durant, R.H. (1998). "Pregnancy and other risk behaviours among adolescent girls in Ohio." Journal of Adolescent Health, 22:50-55.; Sabo, D. et al, (1998). The Women's Sports Foundation Report: Sport and Teen Pregnancy. East Meadow, NY: Women's Sports Foundation.

[27] Artal, M. and Sherman, C. (1998). "Exercise against depression." Physician and Sportsmedicine, 26(10). Available online from http://www.physsportsmed.com/issues/ 1998/1 0Oct/artal.htm.

[28] National Center for Health Statistics. Health, United States, (2002). Hyattsville, MD, 2002.

[29] Calle, E. et al, (2003). "Overweight, obesity, and mortality from cancer in a prospectively studied cohort of U.S. adults." New England Journal of Medicine, Apr 24, 2003. 348(17)1625-1638.

[30] Henshaw, S.K. (2003). U.S. teenage pregnancy statistics with comparative statistics for women aged 20-24. New York: The Alan Guttmacher Institute.; National Campaign to Prevent Teen Pregnancy. (2002). Not just another single issue: Teen pregnancy prevention's link to other critical social issues. Washington, DC: Author.

[31] Centers for Disease Control and Prevention. (2002). "Annual smoking-attributable mortality, years of potential life lost, and economic costs – United States, 1995-1999. "Morbidity and Mortality Weekly Report, 51:300-303.

[32] U.S. Department of Health and Human Services. (2001). Women and smoking: A report of the surgeon general. Rockville: U.S. Department of Health and Human Services, Office of the Surgeon General.

[33] The Commonwealth Fund. (1997). "Survey finds missed opportunities to improve girls' health." Commonwealth Fund Quaretly 3(3). Online. Retrieved   from http://www.cmwf.org/publist/quarterly/fas97qrt.asp?link=6

[34] Schreiber, G.B. et al, (1996)."Weight modification efforts reported by black and white preadolescent girls: National Heart, Lung, and Blood Institute Growth and Health Study." Pediatrics, 98(1): 63-70.

[35] Bunker, L.K. "Life-long Benefits of Youth Sport Participation for Girls and Women." Presented at the Sport Psychology Conference, University of Virginia, Charlottesville, June 22, 1988)

In addition to physical and mental health benefits, the lessons of sport contribute to women's career success. Eighty percent of women identified as key leaders in Fortune 500 companies participated in sports during their childhood and self-identified as having been "tomboys."[36] More than four out of five executive businesswomen (82%) played sports growing up – and the vast majority say lessons learned on the playing field have contributed to their success in business.[37] In a study of active female executives, 86% percent said sports helped them to be disciplined, 69% said sports helped them develop leadership skills that contributed to their professional success, and 69% said sports has given them a competitive edge over others.[38]

NEED FOR CONGRESSIONAL LEADERSHIP

I am here to respectfully request that members of Congress continue and increase their efforts to address the issue of lower opportunities for girls to participate in sports and physical activity. Specifically:

1. The Office of Civil Rights of the Department of Education must enforce Title IX. There are too many institutions that are simply not in compliance with the law and too few compliance reviews are being conducted. Funding and other encouragement for this agency is necessary.

2. Efforts to weaken Title IX should not be supported by Congress. Our sons and daughters must have the same opportunities and encouragement to participate in sports and physical activity.

3. Funding for the Carol M. White Physical Education Program, an act promulgated because of the leadership of Senator Stevens, should be increased in order to provide funds for mandatory physical education programming and meeting state physical education standards. Physical education delivered through our school is most cost effective physical activity delivery system we can invest in and the only program that serves children of all socio-economic levels.

---

[36] Bunker, L.K. "Life-long Benefits of Youth Sport Participation for Girls and Women." Presented at the Sport Psychology Conference, University of Virginia, Charlottesville, June 22, 1988)

[37] Game Face, From the Locker Room to the Boardroom: A Survey on Sports in the Lives of Women Business Executives, Feb. 2002

[38] Women in Higher Education, March 2002.

4. The United States Olympic Committee and its national sports governing bodies must be asked to fulfill the full promise of the Ted Stevens Olympic and Amateur Sports Act to provide equal opportunities for women, minorities and the disabled in grassroots as well as elite level sports. We will not continue to dominate Olympic competition if we forget about broad participation at the grassroots level.

Your consideration of these comments is greatly appreciated.

In: Women in Sports pp. 121-129
Editors: Amelia S. Halloway

ISBN: 978-1-61728-161-7
© 2010 Nova Science Publishers, Inc.

Chapter 9

TESTIMONY OF DONNA DE VARONA, U.S. OLYMPIAN AND SPORTS COMMENTATOR, BEFORE THE COMMITTEE ON COMMERCE, SCIENCE AND TRANSPORTATION ON PROMOTION AND ADVANCEMENT OF WOMEN IN SPORTS

Donna De Varona

Good Morning, I am Donna de Varona. I want to thank the Senate Committee on Commerce, Science and Transportation for inviting me to testify today, and I ask that my written statement and attachments be included in the record.

My relationship with Washington and Congress dates back to the 1960s, when after returning from the 1964 Olympic games in Tokyo, I was appointed to my first of four terms on the President's Council on Physical Fitness. Back then I spent my summers working in intercity programs with children. I have also served on the United States Olympic Committee and the Boards of the Special Olympics, the Women's Sports Foundation, and the U.S. Soccer Foundation. I was a member of President Ford's Commission on Olympic Sports and President Carter's Women's Advisory Commission. From 1976 to

1978, I was a special consultant to the U.S. Senate on sports matters, and most recently I served as a Commissioner on Secretary of Education Roderick Paige's Opportunity in Athletics Commission. Subsequently, I was appointed to a Senate task force to help recommend a comprehensive plan to restructure the United States Olympic Committee.

Today we have been asked to address the status of women in sport both in the areas of promotion and opportunities. Although women and young girls have come a long way since the passage of Title IX some thirty four years ago, there is still a lot to do. The framers of the legislation and later on the guidelines understood that mandating equality in opportunity could not happen overnight, and that is the reason why the guidelines and the three-part participation test are crafted the way they are. The guidelines and the test are flexible and fair. History has painted a picture of tremendous growth and acceptance of the female athlete, but she still battles the perception that girls and women are inherently less interested in sports than men and that providing women with opportunities cheats men out of resources. The argument pits young men and women against each other, and claims like these, as well as widespread non-compliance with Title IX in schools across the country have resulted in women being treated like second-class citizens on the playing field. For example, although on average women are 54% of the students in colleges, they receive only 43% of the sports participation opportunities, 38% of athletic operating dollars and 33% of the money spent on recruitment. At the high school level, girls represent only 42% of varsity athletes. In addition, women and girls continue to face discrimination at all levels of education and in community, recreational and professional sports programs, including in coverage of these programs by the media. With respect to promotion, the lifeblood of any sport, a study of national and regional papers revealed that women receive only about 7 to 9 percent of the space in the sports sections and less than that in air time.

While girls and women can perform on the athletic stage, they still do not run a major sports broadcast network, nor make many important broadcast programming decisions. In educational institutions, the number of women head coaches and sports administrators has stagnated. In the past decade, we have seen two women's sports magazines fold, two professional leagues go out of business, and numerous established women's sports leaders leave the sporting profession. Softball has been taken off the Olympic program. In the broadcast profession, two well-known sports personalities—Robyn Roberts and Hanna Storm—have moved over to news departments. On the collegiate level, many female sports administrators have been let go with no future hope of employment in a sporting world too often controlled by a huge boys' club with sports boosters pulling the strings. For example, take a look at the story of 1972 Olympic gold medalist swimmer, Karen Moe. Karen has spent more than twenty years at the University of California. A winning and honored athlete and coach, she mentored 49 All-Americans and 9 Olympians. Fourteen years ago she was promoted to the athletics department and has consistently been given high performance ratings as an administrator. This year she was let go from her job with no explanation. Her departure is a loss to the University, to the students, and to those women who have lost a role model and are now wondering about pursuing a profession as sports administrator.

Yet with the stunning success of events like the 1999 Women's World Cup, when America's largest and most prestigious stadiums were packed with young vibrant fans to watch women compete, one might get the impression that all is healthy in women's sports. After all, since the passage of Title IX, we have witnessed an unprecedented increase in participation. Before Title IX was enacted, fewer than 32,000 took part in collegiate sports. Now more than 150,000 take part. In high school, the number has gone from 300,000 to over 2.8 million. With this increased participation has come the ability to research the true benefits of sport for women, and the results show huge benefits such as the promotion of responsible social behavior, greater academic success, and increased personal skills. According to published research such as the Carnegie Corporation's "The Role of Sports in Youth Development," compared to their non-athletic peers, athletes are less likely to smoke or use drugs; have lower rates of sexual activity and teen pregnancy; have higher grades; and learn how to work with a team, perform under pressure, set goals, and take criticism. Since health costs are soaring in this country and the nation faces a serious problem with morbid obesity and diabetes, I would be remiss if I did not mention the health benefits to those who are fit and much more able lead by example and teach the values of a healthy lifestyle to their peers and someday their children.

However, it is dangerous to assume that just because some exceptional efforts attract a nationwide spotlight all is healthy in women's sports. In fact, despite the fact that sports for girls and women have proven to be so beneficial, there is still an unfortunate debate going on as to the merits of the law that created those opportunities. In June 2002, a 15 member commission was appointed by Secretary of Education Roderick Paige to review opportunities in athletics. I was a member and I am disappointed to say that most of our time was spent on longstanding Title IX policies governing athletics and whether they should be revised. To this day, I feel that we all missed an important opportunity to address the larger issue of how to provide more sports and fitness opportunities to all students in all our schools. As you have heard from others today, Title IX has been the engine that has created an explosion of sports opportunities for women over the last three decades. But Title IX has also been under constant attack and scrutiny since it was enacted, and today is unfortunately no different. The impetus for the Commission centered on claims by some that the way in which Title IX has always been enforced by the Department "needlessly results in the elimination of some men's teams." The Department spent a year and about $700,000 of taxpayers' money and heard from thousands of experts and citizens nationwide through public meetings, emails, reports, and letters, ultimately adopting 23 recommendations. A USA Today/CNN/Gallup poll conducted during the Commission's tenure indicated that seven of 10 adults who are familiar with Title IX think the federal law should be strengthened or left alone. Yet many of the Commission's ultimate recommendations would have seriously weakened Title IX's protections and substantially reduced the opportunities to which women and girls are entitled under current law.

For this reason, and because the Commission's report failed to address key issues regarding the discrimination women and girls still face in obtaining equal opportunities in athletics, Co-Commissioner Julie Foudy and I released a Minority Report setting forth our views. We felt an obligation to all those who testified to produce a Minority Report because, contrary to what we were promised at the beginning of our deliberations, we were not permitted to include within the Commission's report a full discussion of the issues and our position on the recommendations that were adopted.

In our Minority Report, we pointed out that the Title IX athletics policies have been critical to the effort to expand opportunities for women and girls, have been in place through Republican and Democratic Administrations, and have been upheld unanimously by the federal appellate courts. We also noted that advances for women and girls have not resulted in an overall decrease in opportunities for men, and that in the cases where men's teams have been cut, budgetary decisions and the athletics arms race are the true culprits. Even the Division I athletic directors who served on the Commission testified that revenue producing sports in big-time colleges are "headed for a train wreck." Based on these findings, we recommended that the current Title IX athletics policies not be changed but enforced to eliminate the continuing discrimination against women and girls in athletics. We also recommended that schools and the public be educated about the flexible nature of the law, reminded that cutting men's teams to achieve compliance is not necessary or favored, and encouraged to rein in escalating athletics costs to give more female and male athletes chances to play. The outcome of this lengthy and costly Opportunity in Athletics debate was that the Department of Education rejected the Commission's proposals and strongly reaffirmed the longstanding Title IX athletics policies. In its July 11, 2003 "Further Clarification of Intercollegiate Athletics Policy Guidance Regarding Title IX Compliance," the Department of Education stated: "After eight months of discussion and an extensive and inclusive fact-finding process, the Commission found very broad support throughout the country for the goals and spirit of Title IX. With that in mind, OCR today issues this Further Clarification in order to strengthen Title IX's promise of non-discrimination in the athletic programs of our nation's schools." The document goes on to say that Title IX's three-part participation test provides schools with three separate ways to comply and that nothing in that test requires or encourages schools to cut men's teams; it also promised that OCR would aggressively enforce the longstanding Title IX standards, including implementing sanctions for institutions that do not comply.

However, less than two years after strongly reaffirming the longstanding Title IX athletics policies, and without any notice or public input, the Department of Education did an about-face and posted on its website, late in the afternoon of Friday, March 17, 2005, a new Title IX policy that threatens to reverse the enormous progress women and girls have made in sports since the enactment of Title IX. This new policy, called an "Additional Clarification," creates a major loophole through which schools can evade their obligation to provide equal sports opportunities to women and girls. The bottom line is that the policy allows schools to gauge female students' interest in athletics by doing nothing more than conducting an e-mail survey and to claim—in these days of excessive e-mail spam—that a failure to respond to the survey shows a lack of interest in playing sports. It eliminates schools' obligation to look broadly and proactively at whether they are satisfying women's interests in sports, and will thereby perpetuate the cycle of discrimination to which women have been subjected. The new Clarification violates basic principles of equality, as I explain further below.

As a member of the Commission that spent a year carefully analyzing these issues, I am deeply troubled that the Department would change its 2003 stated position, in which it reaffirmed the longstanding Title IX policies and pledged to enforce them. Instead, the Administration has unilaterally adopted this dangerous new policy without public announcement or opportunity for public comment. Five of my fellow Commissioners and I are so concerned about this new Clarification that we recently sent a letter to athletic administrators around the country warning them about the flaws of the survey procedure endorsed in it, and urging them to decline to use such procedures and instead to join us in asking for it to be withdrawn. To fully understand why this new Clarification is so dangerous, it is important to review the relevant longstanding Title IX athletics policies. Title IX requires schools to provide males and females with equal sports participation opportunities. A 1979 Policy Interpretation elaborates on this requirement by providing three independent ways that schools can meet it – by showing that:

The percentages of male and female athletes are about the same as the percentages of male and female students enrolled in the school (the "proportionality" prong); or

The school has a history and continuing practice of expanding opportunities for the underrepresented sex—usually women.

The school is fully and effectively meeting the athletic interests and abilities of the underrepresented sex. The Department's new Clarification allows schools not meeting the first or second prongs --that is, schools that are not providing equal opportunities to their female students and that have not consistently improved opportunities for them--to show that they are nonetheless in compliance with Title IX by doing nothing more than sending a "model" e-mail survey to their female students asking about their interest in additional sports opportunities. According to the Clarification, the Department will presume that schools comply with Title IX if they use this survey and find insufficient interest to support additional opportunities for women, unless female students can provide "direct and very persuasive evidence" to the contrary.

This new policy dramatically weakens existing law. First, it allows schools to use surveys alone to demonstrate compliance with the law. Under prior Department policies, schools must consider many other factors besides surveys to show compliance with prong three, including: requests by students to add a particular sport; participation rates in club or intramural sports; participation rates in sports in high schools, amateur athletic associations, and community sports leagues in areas from which the school draws its students; and interviews with students, coaches, and administrators. The new Clarification eliminates the obligation to consider these important criteria. Second, surveys are problematic because they are likely only to measure the discrimination that has limited, and continues to limit, sports opportunities for women and girls. Courts have recognized that interest cannot be measured apart from opportunity. In other words, to quote the movie Field of Dreams,

"If you build it, they will come." Basing women's opportunities on their responses to surveys that measure their prior lack of exposure will only perpetuate the cycle of discrimination. The new Clarification is particularly damaging for students in high school, where female students are likely to have had even fewer sports opportunities that would inform their responses to a survey, and where students should be encouraged to try many different sports, not have their opportunities limited by what they might have experienced or be interested in at that time.

Third, by allowing schools to restrict surveys to enrolled and admitted students, the Clarification lets schools off the hook from having to measure interest broadly. The Clarification ignores the reality that students interested in a sport not offered by a school are unlikely to attend that school. By not requiring schools to evaluate interest that exists beyond their own campuses—such as in high school, community, and recreational programs in the areas from which a school typically draws its students—the new policy allows schools to select the universe of people who will be able to respond from those who have already signaled their willingness to accept limited opportunities.

Fourth, the Clarification authorizes flawed survey methodology. For example, schools may e-mail the survey to all female students and interpret a lack of response as evidence of lack of interest. Given the notoriously low response rates to surveys in general, let alone to anything sent via email, this authorization will allow schools to avoid adding new opportunities for women even where interest does in fact exist on campus. In addition, schools may presume that young women's self-assessment of lack of ability to compete at the varsity level reflects an actual lack of ability. Young women who have played sports at the club level or sports other than the ones being considered for varsity status may well have the ability to compete at a varsity level in the sport at issue. Tennis players, for example, may also be able to play squash, and many female athletes can become expert rowers. But under the new Clarification, schools are relieved of any obligation to seek the opinions of coaches or other experts on this issue.

Fifth, the new Clarification shifts the burden to female students to show that they are entitled to equal opportunity. Longstanding Title IX policies put the burden on schools to show that they are fully meeting the interests and abilities of their female students. The new Clarification forces women to prove that their schools are not satisfying their interests and that they are entitled to additional opportunities.

Finally, the Department's new policy does not even require that the Office for Civil Rights monitor schools' use of the survey to ensure that they meet minimal requirements for survey use or interpret the results accurately. For all these reasons, the Department's new Clarification represents a giant step backwards in the progress that women and girls have made in the past three decades. If left in place and used by schools, the new Clarification will lead to a reduction in opportunities for our nation's daughters. We call on Congress to do everything within its power ensure that this does not happen.

Title IX has opened the door for millions of women and girls to participate in sports, but much work remains to be done to fulfill its promise and vision. We welcome Congress' focus on the promotion and advancement of women in sports and look forward to working together to expand athletic opportunities for women and girls.

Footnotes

[1] NCAA, 2002-03 Gender Equity Report (2004).

[2] NFHS, 2002 High School Athletics Participation Survey.

[3] See, e.g., Priest, Laurie and Liane M. Summerfield, "Promoting Gender Equity in Middle and Secondary School Sports Programs," ERIC Digest, 1994; Rebecca Vesely, "California Takes Lead in Sports Equity," Women's eNews, Sept. 13, 2004 (regarding bill banning gender bias in youth athletics programs run by cities and counties), available at http://www.womensenews.org/article.cfm/dyn/aid/1988/context/archive; Sarah J. Murray, "Posting Up in the Pink Ghetto," Women's Sports Foundation, available at http://www.womenssportsfoundation.org/cgi-bin/iowa/issues/body/article.html?record=884.

[4] Judith Jenkins George, "Lack of News Coverage for Women's Athletics: A Questionable Practice of Newspaper Priorities," Aug. 20, 2001, available at http://www. womenssportsfoundation.org/cgi-bin/iowa/issues/media/article.html?record=807.

[5] National Collegiate Athletic Association (NCAA), 1982-2002 Sponsorship and Participation Report 65, available at http://ncaa.org/library/research/participation_rates/1982-2002/participation.pdf; National Federation of State High School Associations (NFHS), 2002 High School Athletics Participation Survey, available at http://www. nfhs.org/nf_survey_resources.asp.

[6] See, e.g., Carnegie Corporation, The Role of Sports in Youth Development 9 (March 1996); NFHS, The Case for High School Activities (2002) at 3, 9; The National Campaign to Prevent Teen Pregnancy, Fact Sheet: Not Just Another Single Issue: Teen Pregnancy and Athletic Involvement (July 2003); The Women's Sports Foundation Report: Sport and Teen Pregnancy (1998) at 5-7; The President's Council on Physical Fitness and Sports, Physical Activity & Sports in the Lives of Girls (Spring 1997); and Black Female Athletes Show Grad-Rate Gains, The NCAA News (June 28, 1995).

[7] See "Open to All": Title IX at Thirty, The Secretary of Education's Commission on Opportunity in Athletics, Feb. 28, 2003, available at http://www.ed.gov/about/bdscomm/list/athletics/report.html.

[8] Erik Brady, "Poll: Most adults want Title IX law left alone." USA TODAY, Jan. 7, 2003.

[9] See Minority Views on the Report of the Commission on Opportunity in Athletics, Report Submitted by Donna de Varona and Julie Foudy, Feb. 2003 (attached).

[10] Office for Civil Rights, United States Department of Education, "Further Clarification of Intercollegiate Athletics Policy Guidance Regarding Title IX Compliance," July 11, 2003 (attached).

[11] Office for Civil Rights, United States Department of Education, "Additional Clarification of Intercollegiate Athletics Policy: Three-Part Test ? Part Three," Mar. 17, 2005 (attached).

[12] "Dear Colleague" Letter from Ted Leland et al., Oct. 11, 2005 (attached).

[13] United States Department of Health, Education, and Welfare, Office for Civil Rights, Title IX of the Education Amendments of 1972; a Policy Interpretation; Title IX and Intercollegiate Athletics, 44 Fed. Reg. 71,413 (December 11, 1979).

[14] United States Department of Education, Office for Civil Rights, Clarification of Intercollegiate Athletics Policy Guidance: The Three-Part Test (Jan. 16, 1996).

[15] Cohen v. Brown University, 101 F.3d 155, 179-80 (1st Cir. 1996).

In: Women in Sports pp. 131-133
Editors: Amelia S. Halloway

ISBN: 978-1-61728-161-7
© 2010 Nova Science Publishers, Inc.

Chapter 10

TESTIMONY OF TARA ERICKSON, BEFORE THE COMMITTEE ON COMMERCE, SCIENCE, AND TRANSPORTATION ON PROMOTION AND ADVANCEMENT OF WOMEN IN SPORTS

Tara Erickson

Good morning Chairman Stevens, Senator Inoyue, and members of the Committee. My name is Tara Erickson, and I am the head coach of the women's soccer team at the University of Oregon. As such, I want to say a special thank you to Senator Smith, who has shown such great support for the University and who has been a strong leader on the issue we're discussing today: Promotion and advancement of women in sports.

Senator Smith you should know that I spent a lot time in your state as a kid, but I grew up in nearby Puyallup, Washington and played soccer in high school. I was fortunate enough to earn a scholarship to the University of Washington and play for Lesle Gallimore, the woman who helped guide my career. I earned a bachelor's degree in communications, but my first love remained soccer. When I graduated, there were more opportunities for me to play professional soccer in Europe than there were in the United States. I still loved playing, and I played in Germany for a year, but I wanted to come home to the Pacific Northwest.

Coach Gallimore at UW convinced me to consider a career in coaching. I earned a position on her staff, and once again Coach Gallimore became my mentor. I went on to my own head coaching job at Portland State, and now I'm at the University of Oregon. As a coach I have been very fortunate to share my love of sport with my teammates. Coaching is a gift, and I do not take this blessing lightly. Players that I have coached have gone on to become productive members of our community, and I hope have also become ambassadors of opportunity and fair play. As a coach, I strive to always give as much on the sidelines as I did as a player. The kids deserve that, as does the institution I represent.

But sometimes fair play and opportunity need an extra push and that's why I am a huge supporter of Title IX. This important civil rights law has helped establish a level of fairness and equity in athletics. The law's impact, however, has extended far beyond the classrooms and the athletic fields. It has created an entire generation of mentors who work with young girls – and young boys. It has nurtured interest in sports to the point where the athletes sitting with me this morning have become the pride of our nation and the envy of the rest of the world. It has created economic opportunities and job security for people like me – soccer may be played today by younger women like the amazing Cat Reddick, but I'm still earning a living working with the game I love so much. Most importantly, it helps parents teach a simple yet powerful lesson to children – a lesson I will soon teach my adorable baby boy, Maklain: when it comes to sports, EVERYONE deserves a chance to play.

We know sports have a positive impact on girls' lives. Studies show that girls who participate in sports are less likely to smoke or use drugs. They perform better in the classroom. Just this past November our team honored Caitlin Gamble, a midfielder and the first Academic All-American in our program's history. They have fewer health problems later in life. They learn how to work with teammates and can develop a feeling of confidence and a sense of purpose. I'm proud to know that as a coach and a mentor, I can help young women in this way.

I am so very proud to be part of the University of Oregon. The University does a great job making sure the opportunities we provide our male athletes are mirrored by the opportunities we provide our young women. They do more than simply follow the letter of the law; they embrace its spirit. Without Title IX, we don't know if there would be a women's soccer coach at Oregon, or Portland State, or Washington, or anywhere else. I can't imagine what my life would be like without the opportunities I had.

One of the things I enjoy most about my job at the University of Oregon is speaking with women and girls who visit us. Playing college athletics was one of the best experiences of my life, but it's even better for young women today. I love to share the experiences of what sports meant to me as an athlete in high school and at the University of Washington. I can see the excitement in the eyes of young athletes as you realize you're connecting with them. I can see the pride in the faces of their mothers as they think about the first- rate education their daughters can obtain here. Thanks in no small part to the fact that our soccer program was awarded two more scholarships, I feel the joy of knowing that an opportunity awaits that young girl who has worked so hard to get to this point. And I also appreciate that it wasn't always like this. If we lower the threshold for compliance with Title IX, those young women will still have the athleticism but may not have the opportunity. It's that simple.

I cannot begin to tell you how proud I am that the young athletes here this morning are choosing to speak out in support of opportunities for girls and women in sport. It's easy to look at the progress we've made and say we don't need Title IX any more. But we can't look back. We must make sure the generations of mentors don't stop with the incredible athletes – the wonderful young women – here today. Please fight to give young girls the opportunity to excel in anything they choose. Please fight to help them have confidence and purpose. Help them choose to participate. Help them be athletes. Help them be mentors. Help them be strong.

If you keep Title IX strong, you won't be alone. Companies like Nike have helped support women's sports at every level. Specifically, Nike helps raise visibility and awareness of women's sports so the youngsters who play sports have role models to follow and dreams to pursue. In addition to its support for women's professional athletes, the company sponsored its first-annual Nike Women's Marathon in San Francisco in October 2004 in celebration of the 20th anniversary of women's first participation in the Olympic Games marathon.

So I thank you very much for giving me the opportunity to speak with you this morning. I want to thank Senator Smith again for being such a stalwart leader on civil rights issues. I share the pride that we all have in the young women who have joined us. I know the title of the hearing is the promotion and advancement of women in sports, but you must know that Title IX made this hearing and my testimony possible. And like these amazing women, please fight to keep Title IX strong.

In: Women in Sports pp. 135-138
Editors: Amelia S. Halloway

ISBN: 978-1-61728-161-7
© 2010 Nova Science Publishers, Inc.

Chapter 11

STATEMENT OF JENNIE FINCH, OLYMPIC GOLD MEDALIST SOFTBALL PLAYER, BEFORE THE COMMITTEE ON COMMERCE, SCIENCE AND TRANSPORTATION ON PROMOTION AND ADVANCEMENT OF WOMEN IN SPORTS

Jennie Finch

I am Jennie Finch, currently a member of the National Pro Fastpitch Chicago Bandits women's softball team. I was the pitcher for the gold medal winning 2004 United States women's Olympic softball team. I played softball at the University of Arizona and hold the NCAA record for consecutive wins (60). In my senior season, I helped Arizona reach the NCAA Women's College World Series and place second. In 2001, Arizona won the national championship and I was named the Women's College World Series Most Outstanding Player. As Pac-10 Pitcher of the Year, I finished that season with a 32-0 record and the NCAA record for most wins in a season without a defeat. I am a two-time winner of the Honda Award, an award presented to the nation's best player. I am also involved with the Make-A-Wish Foundation and give clinics and lessons to underserved kids.

I would not be here if it wasn't for Title IX. Like my two older brothers, my life has been centered around sports. It is where I have met my closest friends and shaped the values that have made me a successful athlete, student and role model for young people. I started playing softball when I was five years old and was so excited to get introduced to a sport just for girls. It made me what I am: a disciplined and hardworking person at whatever I do, a team player who understands the importance of working with others, and a person who knows how to put losing, sitting the bench or a tough boss in perspective. I know I was lucky in that I had access to many opportunities that other women did not. I grew up with people who supported my playing. I had access to neighborhood teams. My family provided enough financial support for me to play in after school programs that many girls either couldn't afford or didn't have the transportation to enable them to play. I had an athletic scholarship that gave me a college education and sports career opportunities. I had female role models to look up to starting in middle school, athletes like Julie Foudy and Mia Hamm who made me realize that there was room in the world of sports for women. They ignited my dream of becoming an Olympic athlete. Seeing women on television was very important to me. It opened my eyes to the possibilities of women's sports. It showed me what I could do and who I could be. And now I'm a professional athlete with the opportunity to make my living through sport as so many men have been able to do before me.

But there are others who have not been as fortunate as I.

- Girls comprise 49.03% of the high school population (National Center for Education Statistics (NCES), 2003-2004) but only receive 41.3% of all athletic participation opportunities. (National Federation of High Schools (NFHS), 2004-2005)
- Females comprise 57% of the college student population (NCES, Fall 2002) but only receive 43% of all college athletic participation opportunities. (National Collegiate Athletic Association (NCAA), 2003-2004)
- College female athletes receive $135 million or 25% fewer scholarship dollars than college male athletes. (NCAA Gender Equity Report, 2002-2003)
- College female athletes receive $1.18 billion or 80.21% fewer sport operating budget dollars than college male athletes. (NCAA Gender Equity Report, 2002-2003)

- NCAA colleges spend $39 million or 103% fewer dollars recruiting female athletes than they do on male athletes. (NCAA Gender Equity Report, 2002-2003)

Women are vastly underrepresented in sports industry and sports leadership positions:

College Positions	Male	Female
Athletic Directors	81.5%	18.5%
Head Coaches of Women's Teams	55.9%	44.1%
Head Coaches of Men's Teams	98%	2%
Full-time Athletic Trainers	70%	30.0%
Sports Information Directors	87.8%	12.2%
--Acosta and Carpenter, 2004		

Sports-Industry Careers	Male	Female
Big 4 leagues	87.4%	12.6%
Other leagues/teams	82.9%	17.1%
Sports marketing agencies	71.7%	28.3%
Broadcast/media	91.7%	8.3%
Stadium/arena/track	82.5%	17.5%
Corporations/manufacturers	78.3%	21.7%
--Sports Business Journal 2002 Salary Survey		

Sports-Industry Careers	Persons of Color
Big 4 leagues	7.6%
Other leagues/teams	6.1%
Sports marketing agencies	6.6%
Broadcast/media	4.2%
Stadium/arena/track	5.3%
College	9.3%
Corporations/manufacturers	17.4%
-- Sports Business Journal 2002 Salary Survey	

In general, the higher the status or salary of the position, the lower the percentage of females who are employed. Women of color are in double jeopardy with regard to sports industry employment, facing race as well as gender discrimination. We have so far to go.

It's been 34 years since the passage of Title IX and 28 years since the passage of the Ted Stevens Olympic and Amateur Sports Act. Yet, discrimination still exists in schools, colleges and amateur sports. This discrimination is readily apparent to the public in my own sport. Baseball teams in high schools all over the nation play on-campus, on manicured fields with lights, dugouts, batting cages, locker rooms and toilet facilities while girls' teams are relegated to inferior public park fields with no amenities.

Just this past year, despite the fact that women are still significantly underrepresented in the Olympic Games, the International Olympic Committee voted to eliminate women's softball from the 2012 Games. There are few women in leadership positions in softball's national or international sport governing bodies despite the Ted Stevens Act which mandates that such opportunities be provided.

Women's sport in general is virtually ignored by the press, receiving less than 7% of all sports coverage in the print and electronic media. If a female athlete chooses to be a mother, we are pushed out of sports because there are no support structures or player benefits to accommodate players with children. This is particularly important to me because I am expecting a son in April.

Please know that I'm not here to complain. Rather, I am here to ask that members of Congress address these issues because it is very difficult for athletes and parents to do so. We have the federal mechanism in place to realize the promise of equal opportunity in sport if Congress makes sure that Title IX enforcement and oversight of the USOC and its national sport governing bodies happens.

Sport is too potent a force in society and has too much of an impact on an individual's health, confidence and self-esteem for us not to do everything we can to ensure that sports girls and sportswomen are treated as well as sports boys and sportsmen.

Your consideration of these comments is greatly appreciated.

In: Women in Sports pp. 139-143
Editors: Amelia S. Halloway

ISBN: 978-1-61728-161-7
© 2010 Nova Science Publishers, Inc.

Chapter 12

TESTIMONY OF CHRISTINE GRANT, FORMER ATHLETIC DIRECTOR AT THE UNIVERSITY OF IOWA AND ASSOCIATE PROFESSOR IN THE DEPARTMENT OF HEALTH AND SPORTS STUDIES, BEFORE THE COMMITTEE ON COMMERCE, SCIENCE AND TRANSPORTATION ON PROMOTION AND ADVANCEMENT OF WOMEN IN SPORTS

Christine Grant

Chairman Stevens, Ranking Member Inouye and other distinguished members of the Committee, thank you for inviting me to testify before you today.

I am Christine Grant, former Athletic Director for our separate women's athletic department at the University of Iowa for 27 years and currently an Associate Professor in the Department of Health and Sport Studies.

Today I would like to do three things: (1) present you with some facts and figures that describe the progress we have made since 1972 for women in sport in our nation, (2) briefly describe some financial trends, especially in football and men's basketball at the intercollegiate level, and (3) note areas where institutions in specific divisions are doing well and where institutions in divisions need to consider providing additional support.

In slide 1, the growth of girls' participation at the high school level since 1971 has risen to 42% of the athletic population. However, it is also important to note that boys' participation numbers have also increased significantly, from 3.7million to over 4 million. Today, boys still have 58% of all athletic opportunities.

The trend of increasing participation slots for men is also seen at the intercollegiate level. In the NCAA, men in 1989 had approximately 176,000 opportunities, and by 2004 that number had increased by about 42,000.

There is a myth circulating around the nation that Title IX has caused the demise of some men's sports, specifically wrestling and gymnastics. Yet the next slide shows that there has actually been a significant and steady decline in the popularity of these two sports since the early 1980s. You will recall that in the decade of the 1980s, Title IX did not apply to athletics for a period of 4 years due to the Supreme Court's decision in *Grove City College v. Bell.*[1] Additionally, there was little, if any, enforcement of the law even when it was restored in 1988 when Congress passed the Civil Rights Restoration Act of 1987.[2] So, the fact that many teams were lost in the 80s is not because of Title IX. The reality is that the popularity of specific sports changes over the years. For example, look at the increase in the number of football teams and soccer teams in that same time frame. Between these two sports, 333 teams were added for men; teams that were lost in wrestling and gymnastics totaled 182.

I also decided to track what was happening in women's gymnastics. As you see, the declining popularity of that sport is clearly apparent.

The General Accounting Office was asked to do an in-depth study of participation opportunities in both the NCAA and the NAIA. Their results show that in an 18 year period, there was a net gain of 36 teams for men, which constituted a 5% increase in participation.

That trend was supported by the data from the NCAA. Between 1988 and 2002, there was a net increase of 61 men's teams. After further research, however, I discovered that while Divisions II and III had experienced net gains for men's teams, Division I had experienced a net loss. Upon further investigation, I discovered that it was in Division 1-A where the greatest net losses had occurred. This is surprising since these institutions have by far the

---

[1] 465 U.S. 555 (1984).
[2] Pub. L. 100-259, 102 Stat. 28 (1988).

largest budgets. Time does not allow me to expand on this issue except to say that I believe that million-dollar salaries for football and men's basketball, coupled with an arms race in the building of superb facilities, may well be related to the loss of some men's sports in Division I-A. For example, at Iowa, last year we paid our football coach over $2 million; we paid the President of the University $300,000.

The next slide shows the enormous population from which we recruit our intercollegiate athletes. Only 163,000 female student-athletes currently get the chance to compete at the university level. Obviously, we could add hundreds of women's teams from this large population. If we are not adding sports at the collegiate level, it is not because of a lack of interest or ability.

Tracking the financial situation for the last thirty years shows that the lack of progress toward increased financial support for women was not caused by lack of money; it was caused by lack of commitment. The money was there; the commitment was not. In Division I-A, for every new dollar that went to women's sport after 1972 till 1993, three new dollars went to men's sports. Let me repeat that: for every new dollar that went to women's sports, three new dollars went to men's sport. Since 1993, for every new dollar spent on women's sports, two new dollars have gone to men's sports. This allocation is not a trend that lends itself to creating equal opportunities and comparable treatment for our female student-athletes. On the contrary, it exacerbates the problem.

In 1993, a new researcher decided to try to factor out the administrative costs. You will note that while the expenses of men's athletics currently are more than double those for women, the administrative costs also far exceed the costs for women's programs.

A troubling trend is the increasing expenditures in football and men's basketball. You will note in the next slide that men's football expenditures have increased three fold since 1985 and men's basketball expenses almost four fold.

At the same time, the deficits in athletic programs have been increasing at a rate that is extremely troubling. In Division I-A, the average deficit has doubled in ten years to $4.4 million. This is at a time when universities as a whole are struggling to finance academic programs. All other divisions are facing the same trend in deficits.

This leads us to examine the expenditures of football and men's basketball, In 1985, the budgets for these two sports took up almost half of the men's athletic budget - 49%. In the latest financial analysis, these two sports now consume almost three quarters of the men's budget - 74%.

Where does that leave men's so called "minor" sports? On the short end. Let me rephrase what is happening; football with an average squad of 117 in Division I-A is spending about half a percentage point on each student-athlete for a total of 56% of the men's budget; basketball with 15 players is spending over 1% on each student-athlete for a total of 18% of the men's budget. The other men's sports have only 21 % of the budget for as many as 200 student-athletes. It is not Title IX that is causing this problem; it is the insatiable appetites of football and men's basketball.

The latest NCAA Gender Equity figures show that in the area of participation, Division I has been offering a greater percentage of opportunities. In Division I-A, the percentage of female athletes is 8% below the percentage of female undergraduates, and in Division I-AAA, it is 7% below the percentage of female undergraduates. However, it is clear that those in Division I-AA, II and III need to address this issue to determine if their institutions are being responsive to the increasing interests and abilities of their female students.

In the area of scholarships, the figures are better, but that is because they only have to match the participation rates, which, as I mentioned above, are still below where they should be.

In recruiting, Division I-A is well behind the other divisions and sub-divisions. This is an area that needs a lot of attention.

So too is the disparity in Division I-A in the total expense column. Division I-A is 14% behind the participation ratio while the other subdivisions and divisions are doing well. Again, it appears that the most lucrative programs in the nation are not committed to equitable treatment for male and female student-athletes.

The final slide shows a 2003 Poll by the Wall Street Journal and NBC News. It notes that 68% of the public approve of Title IX. What is more surprising to many is the result that "cutting back on men's athletics to ensure equivalent athletic opportunities for women" received a 66% approval rating. The public recorded a 70% rating for strengthening the law or making no changes to the law.

In conclusion, the facts show that both men's and women's opportunities to play sports have increased since Title IX was enacted in 1972, with men and boys still receiving more opportunities than women and girls today. While some men's and women's teams have decreased in number, this decline is not because of Title IX, but rather because the popularity of specific sports changes over the years for various reasons. With respect to expenditures, educational institutions are not even close to providing equal financial support to women, and men's budgets are being dominated by football and basketball, which leaves little money for all other men's teams. The recruiting budgets for female athletes are particularly dismal and need to be increased. Title IX and other gender equity laws must be strongly enforced if we are to continue moving forward towards true equality for women and girls in sports.

In: Women in Sports pp. 145-147
Editors: Amelia S. Halloway

ISBN: 978-1-61728-161-7
© 2010 Nova Science Publishers, Inc.

Chapter 13

TESTIMONY OF LYNETTE MUND, WEST FARGO, NORTH DAKOTA, BEFORE THE COMMITTEE ON COMMERCE, SCIENCE AND TRANSPORTATION ON PROMOTION AND ADVANCEMENT OF WOMEN IN SPORTS

Lynette Mund

Good morning, Chairman Stevens, Senator Inouye and Members of the Committee. On behalf of the state of North Dakota, I would like to thank the Commerce Committee for hearing my testimony.

My name is Lynette Mund and I am a teacher and head girls basketball coach at West Fargo High School in West Fargo, North Dakota. I am here today to testify to the importance of women's athletics and the struggles of providing athletic opportunities to young girls in rural communities. I will also discuss what I am doing to encourage more young girls to participate in sports in North Dakota.

Girls and women being involved in athletics has been a long discussed issue. Many questions have been asked, such as "Can girls' bodies handle it?" "Are girls mentally tough enough?" "Does it really make a difference in a girl's life?" I am here as evidence that the answers to the previous questions are all "Yes". The fact that I am in Washington D.C. testifying in front of the

U.S. Senate Commerce Committee shows what a difference sports can make in a girl's life. Twenty years ago, I was a 12 year-old girl who was milking cows on my parent's dairy farm in rural North Dakota, and now I am here in our nation's capitol with some of the most influential people in our country listening to what *I* have to say. I have always loved sports, but I had no idea where they would take me and the confidence they would give me.

At age 13, I was a skinny 8th grader who was stepping out on the basketball court to start my first varsity game, and by age 23, I was a 3-time NCAA Division II National Champion and a college graduate from North Dakota State University who had the confidence to leave ND and move to the "big city" of St. Louis, MO. However, while I was in St. Louis, I always had a desire to move back to ND and give back part of what I had been given. That opportunity presented itself when I was offered the head girls basketball coaching position at West Fargo High School. Being back in ND not only afforded me the chance to work with female athletes in West Fargo, but I was also able to continue working with young girls back near my hometown of Milnor, ND which has a population of 700 people.

As I stated earlier, I grew up on a dairy farm. I was a relatively naïve young lady without much self-confidence. I had always dreamed of going to college, but I knew it would not be affordable without a college scholarship. I remember standing out in the milk barn and hearing on the radio that a local basketball star, Pat Smykowski, had gotten a college scholarship to play basketball, and right then and there I knew that was what I wanted to do. Thankfully, due to the efforts of many great women before me, the chance to participate in college athletics was available; something my mother and many women from her generation never had an opportunity to do. My mom used to talk about wanting to play sports but not having the chance to compete. I sometimes sit and wonder how different my life would be without athletics. I wonder if I would have had the money to attend college, if I would have had the confidence to move away from my home state, and if I would have had the nerve to fly to Washington D.C. all by myself and speak in front of U.S. Senators. However, all of these things happened because I participated in athletics. As a result, I want to inform and inspire other young girls from rural ND.

One of the biggest challenges in rural North Dakota is that there are very few opportunities for athletes to improve their skills. That is why over the last 12 years, I have offered over 40 basketball camps in ND and MN. I am proud to have given over 800 young women the opportunity to participate in their first basketball camp. For many of these young girls, my camps are the only exposure they will have to an athletic camp for the whole year. Over the years, I have had the chance to see some of my former campers continue their careers in high school athletics, some of which I have actually had to coach against! However, it was always worth it to see how far these young ladies have come and the confidence they now carry. At the time they attended camp, you should have seen their eyes when I told them they could have the chance to play in high school or college someday. Some of these girls did not even realize this was an option for them. By exposing these young girls to athletics at an early age, it allows them to see that sports *is* an option. This is relevant to the future of women's athletics because equal access to sports in college only works if girls have the opportunity to get involved in athletics at an early age.

Getting these young ladies involved is even more evident when I look at athletic participation numbers for girls in ND. According to figures from the 2004-2005 North Dakota High School Activities Association, females made up 49 percent of the student population in North Dakota. However, only 40 percent of the student-athletes were females. It is one of my goals to bring this number closer to 49 percent. This is important to me because I have first hand knowledge of how athletics can have a positive effect on a young woman.

I have been very fortunate to coach camps along with a high school basketball team. This year, I have 3 seniors at West Fargo who will be receiving athletic scholarships and playing college basketball next fall. I have had the chance to watch these young ladies grow and mature since their freshman year. They exude a confidence that was not there 3 years ago. They know they have the ability to do whatever they want in life and the self-assurance they will be successful.

By providing my basketball camps and coaching high school basketball, I hope that other young girls from my home state realize that there are many opportunities to participate in athletics, and even a young girl from a town of less than 1000 people can be a National Champion, a college graduate, and a successful, confident professional.

Thank you very much for your time.

In: Women in Sports pp. 149-151
Editors: Amelia S. Halloway

ISBN: 978-1-61728-161-7
© 2010 Nova Science Publishers, Inc.

Chapter 14

TESTIMONY OF CATHERINE ANNE REDDICK, BEFORE THE COMMITTEE ON COMMERCE, SCIENCE AND TRANSPORTATION ON PROMOTION AND ADVANCEMENT OF WOMEN IN SPORTS

Catherine Anne Reddick

Thank you Chairman Stevens, Senator Inouye and members of the Committee. My name is Cat Reddick, and I am thrilled to have the opportunity to speak with you today about an issue that means a great deal to me. Today's hearing is very important – not just to me, but to millions of girls and women who deserve the opportunity to play sports. I want you all to know how much I appreciate your leadership in bringing us all together.

I believe very strongly that if it weren't for an important civil rights law we call Title IX, I probably wouldn't be here today. As you know, that's the law that says schools have to provide the same kinds of opportunities to girls that they do to boys in everything they do, including sports.

I grew up in Birmingham, Alabama, and I've been interested in sports for about as long as I can remember. My father played football for Virginia Tech, so my parents always wanted sports to be a part of my life. I've always enjoyed watching the football powerhouses in the South, like Georgia and

Florida. And of course, in Alabama, the one question you're always asked is about the football game we call the "Iron Bowl" – are you supporting Alabama or Auburn?

It's no stretch to say that when you're talking about sports in Alabama, you're usually talking about football. And as I said, I'm a big fan, too. However, too often growing up, the story would end there. I wanted to play sports, and I had the support of my parents, but opportunities were limited. I had to play on boys' soccer teams until my freshman year of high school. Being the only girl on my team wasn't always easy. Not all of my teammates wanted me there.

I was so happy to play organized sports with other girls in school because it created so many possibilities for me. I'm very fortunate to have gone on to much success. I've had the chance to go to an outstanding college that I wouldn't have been able to afford without an athletic scholarship. I've been on a national championship team. I've traveled to places that many young girls in Birmingham can only dream about. I've had the support of sponsors like Nike who have taken a strong stand for women's sports and Title IX. I've had the privilege to represent our country in the Olympics and play on a team with women who are already national icons. But the most important experiences to me have nothing to do with championships or medals. The best things I've gained from playing sports are the same things that any girl can gain by simply participating.

I've gained self-confidence. I've embraced a healthy lifestyle. I've gained the experience of being part of a team. I've built friendships that will last forever. And I've learned about hard work, patience, and perseverance from the role models of the generation before me – the first generation of athletes to benefit from Title IX. And just as pioneers such as Coach Erickson and many of the other people you will hear from today have done, it's now my obligation and my passion to ensure the opportunities I had are available to the generation of girls that follow me.

Soccer isn't the only thing in my life, but it's an important part. And the lessons I've learned are things I apply to everything in life. That's why this is so important – while not every girl can have a scholarship, they deserve to learn these lessons and improve their lives.

Please understand that this isn't easy. Even today, I have friends – mostly men – who think that Title IX should be limited. Where I'm from, some people still see football and basketball as the only sports that matter, and see women as somehow not worthy or able to participate in sports. However, I also want to say I'm very proud of the progress we've made. When I was growing up in Alabama, there wasn't much information available for girls' soccer, but now interest in the sport is growing faster there than virtually anywhere in the country. The opportunities created by Title IX have generated enough interest and support in girls' soccer that club teams are in full swing in Alabama today.

The interest in sports that Title IX helped create has also attracted positive involvement from companies. Women's athletics is now big business, and that contributes to a healthy economy. The women's fitness industry alone is worth $13 billion worldwide today and is growing rapidly.

It also provides a great opportunity for companies to do the right thing. I'm very proud that Nike, one of my sponsors, is one such company.

Throughout its 33-year history, Nike has worked to inspire the spirit of girls and women by championing change and contributing to a level playing field for female sports. Nike has strived to be at the forefront of cultivating the positive relationship between women and sports and the empowerment the powerful combination catalyzes.

Among Nike's earliest female-focused ads, which ran in 1984, was a series of print ads intended to persuade the International Olympic Committee (IOC) to lift its rule prohibiting women from running in races longer than 1,500 meters. The campaign was successful, and Joan Benoit Samuelson became the first woman to win the Olympic marathon in the 1984 Olympics held in Los Angeles.

In 1995, Nike launched its famous television commercial, "If You Let Me Play." The provocative ad featured young girls citing the importance of being allowed to participate in sports with statistics such as "If you let me play, I will be 60 percent less likely to get breast cancer; I will suffer less depression, if you let me play sports. I will be more likely to leave a man who beats me." The ad was seen by 73 million viewers.

So that's what brings me here this morning. I want you to know that without Title IX, I don't think this would have been possible. I always had the desire to play sports, but I couldn't learn these important lessons until I had the opportunity. I urge you to fight to keep this important civil rights law strong and make sure it's enforced. This is not the time to weaken the rule of fair play. Title IX has done so much for so many young girls. Somewhere in Alabama right now, there's a young girl who has the ability to improve her own life and inspire yet another generation through sports. Please make sure she has the opportunity.

Thank you very much.

In: Women in Sports pp. 153-164
Editors: Amelia S. Halloway

ISBN: 978-1-61728-161-7
© 2010 Nova Science Publishers, Inc.

Chapter 15

STATEMENT OF DOROTHY "DOT" G. RICHARDSON, M.D., VICE-CHAIR, PRESIDENT'S COUNCIL ON PHYSICAL FITNESS AND SPORTS, BEFORE THE COMMITTEE ON COMMERCE, SCIENCE AND TRANSPORTATION ON PROMOTION AND ADVANCEMENT OF WOMEN IN SPORTS

Dorothy "Dot" G. Richardson

Good morning Senator Stevens, Senator Inouye, Committee Members, staff and guests. Thank you for holding this very important hearing.

My name is Dot Richardson, and I'm here today as vice chair of the President's Council on Physical Fitness and Sports to testify about the importance of promoting and advancing opportunities for women in physical activity and sports. I bring you warm greetings from Secretary Michael O. Leavitt of the U.S. Department of Health and Human Services (HHS). The President's Council on Physical Fitness and Sports, an advisory committee within HHS, is celebrating its 50th anniversary in 2006. The observance of the Council's first fifty years (1956-2006) coincides with the tenth anniversary of the Surgeon General's landmark report on physical activity (1996), *Physical*

Activity and Health. Given the rates of overweight and obesity that continue to plague the nation, 2006 presents an opportune time to bring more visibility to the importance of physical activity, fitness and sports for improving and maintaining health.

I feel fortunate to be serving on the Council under the fittest president in our nation's history. President and Mrs. Bush are excellent role models in health and fitness for all Americans. Despite their busy schedules, they make physical activity a regular part of their daily lives. President Bush says, "Better health is an individual responsibility and an important national goal."

To fulfill the vision of a "HealthierUS," the President, the Secretary and the members of the President's Council on Physical Fitness and Sports are asking each American to adopt four simple behaviors than can change your life: be physically active every day; eat a nutritious diet; get preventive screenings; and make healthy choices.

Our nation's poor eating habits and sedentary lifestyles are killing thousands of Americans every day. The cost of obesity and type 2 diabetes combined is up to $250 billion a year. If there were a medication on the market that conveyed all of the health benefits of active living, everyone would take it. To all Americans of all ages and abilities, men and women, boys and girls alike, we say, "Daily physical activity is a magic pill."

I'm here today to tell you the story of a young girl in the late 1960s and early 1970s. She played outdoors with her brothers; she loved to run after rabbits and race trucks, to climb trees, to catch a ball. She shared a frustration with many girls her age: she loved sports but couldn't find a girls' team anywhere. For a young girl at that time, the only way you could play is if a boys' team let you.

One day, that young girl was playing catch with her brother—helping him warm up before he went to play a Little League baseball game. Her brother's coach saw her playing and asked if she wanted to play on the team. But if she did, he said, she'd have to cut her hair short, and he'd call her "Bob."

I was that little girl, Senators. But I wasn't brought up to be a covert operative. So, well-brought up young lady that I was, I smiled and politely declined, then walked over to a nearby field, where there was a team of women practicing softball. The coach noticed me and let me take a few ground balls. I'd never heard of women's fast-pitch softball, but at the age of ten, I became the youngest member of that team.

I was one of the lucky girls back then, able to live my sports dream during my growing-up years. Today, an American girl doesn't have to search as long and hard as I did to belong to a team. There are many chances for girls to play on an organized girls' softball team, from church leagues to recreational leagues. During all my years playing women's softball, I never dreamed I'd experience Olympic glory. But in the summer of 1996, I had the privilege of playing on the team that won a gold medal in women's softball.

That same year, 1996, the Surgeon General published the landmark report *Physical Activity and Health*. That report clearly documented that regular, preferably daily, routine of at least 30 to 60 minutes of brisk walking, bicycling, or even dancing will reduce the risks of developing or dying from cardiovascular disease, breast and colon cancer, and type 2 diabetes and will reduce symptoms of anxiety and depression; help control weight; and help build and maintain healthy bones, muscles and joints. The 30 to 60 minutes doesn't have to be done at one time—it can be broken up into smaller increments.

On the heels of the Surgeon General's report on physical activity and health, the President's Council on Physical Fitness and Sports published its own report, "Physical Activity and Sport in the Lives of Girls: Physical and Mental Health Dimensions from an Interdisciplinary Approach." Today I want to paraphrase some of the highlights of that landmark report and update you on the current work of the U.S. Department of Health and Human Services in addressing physical activity for women and girls in America. Physical activity and sports involvement are important developmental opportunities for both boys and girls. Contributions include increased strength and power, better cardiovascular functioning, enhanced immune system responses, opportunities to develop moral reasoning, positive self-concepts and social interaction skills. There are however unique dimensions of the sport experience for girls in terms of physiological and psychological/emotional development and the challenges, which sometimes exist between socially, influenced expectations.

All children should participate in regular physical activity and sport experiences, especially in quality, adult supervised activities at home, at school and in after- school programs. A wide range of activities should be available, including both individual and group experiences and cooperative vs. competitive ones. Moderate and regular physical activity can promote psychological and emotional well being, including reduced depression. Equal and safe opportunities and environments should be provided for both boys and girls to participate in a full range of physical fitness and sport activities.

Maintaining physical fitness and developing good fundamental movement skills by actively participating in daily activity contributes to happier and healthier lives by facilitating both physical and emotional health.

Involvement in sport and physical activity contributes to the physical movement capacities of girls, the health status of their bodies, the values and ethical behaviors they develop and their personal development of a unique identity. Childhood activities related to sport and physical activity should include opportunities for girls to develop fundamental fitness, and to acquire the motor skills necessary for lifelong learning and leisure time activities and to facilitate good immune system functioning, build physical fitness, and maintain appropriate body weight.

One of the most basic benefits of physical activity is the development of motor skills. Providing these opportunities to learn these skills is important for all people, including all girls and women.

All areas of fitness are affected by regular physical activity but three that seem to be especially impacted by regular physical activity are muscular fitness, cardiovascular fitness (aerobic fitness) and anaerobic power. For most girls, muscular fitness increases until about age 14, but for sedentary girls it may slow more rapidly or even decrease (Blimkie, 1989). However, systematic physical activity including both short term training programs (Sale, 1989) and regular physical activity programs can produce marked improvement in strength for girls.

One of the primary advantages of active physical participation for children seems to be directly linked to lower body fat and a better ratio of lean to fat mass. Children with above average levels of body fat generally have higher total cholesterol, and LDL cholesterol and often-associated elevated blood pressure (Williams, et al., 1992). Elevated levels of cholesterol in children are very important because children who have higher levels of cholesterol are almost three times more likely than older children to have high cholesterol levels as adults (National Cholesterol Education Program, 1991). The best strategy for lowering cholesterol in children is a combination of physical activity and diet which may also lead to lowered blood pressure, and other benefits thought to be brought about because of decreased cardiac output, decreased peripheral resistance, and reduced risk of blood clotting (Blair, et al., 1996).

Physical activity and sport experiences can also be beneficial in maintaining appropriate body weight, or the balance between energy expenditure and caloric intake (especially the relative proportion of fat intake in terms of the percent of total calories. The problem of juvenile obesity is twice as great today as it was in the 1960's (Blair et al., 1996), and a particular problem for juvenile girls. For most young girls, normal daily activity provides an adequate balance of intake and expenditures, but for females with weight problems, maintaining regular physical activity levels is an important adjunct in weight control because of its role in facilitating fat-free mass and promoting the loss of fat (Wells, 1991). It is also thought to be important in reducing the risk of non-insulin dependent diabetes, which is one of the ten most prevalent causes of death in the United States (Blair, et al., 1996).

One major advantage of physical activity for girls is that it increases "peak bone mass." Peak bone mass is the level of bone mass at its highest point– usually occurring in the teens or early 20s. High peak bone mass can be viewed much as a bank savings account where withdrawals can be made later in life when needed. The higher the peak mass, the less likely that losses later in life will result in low bone mass or osteoporosis.

Extensive research has emerged to support the contention that regular physical activity (at a moderate level) facilitates the body's ability to fight infection (e.g. upper respiratory infection (Nieman, 1994)) and disease through increased immune system function (Freedson &Bunker, 1997).

The involvement of girls in sport is largely impacted by the attitudes of parents and other role models (teachers, family). If parents support their involvement and encourage it, girls can benefit in many positive ways from sport and physical activity. There appears to be a strong interaction between how girls perceive their success in sport, and how others influence that perception. During early years, both boys and girls are about equal in terms of physical skills and rely on adult comments (especially parents) to help them judge their competency until about age 10 (Weiss &Ebbeck, 1996). Most girls participate in sport to have fun, improve skills, be with friends and become physically fit while enjoying the challenges and being successful (Weiss &Petlichkoff, 1989). In particular, when motivation to participate in sport was examined, Gill (1992) found three different reasons: competitiveness, win orientation and goal orientation. Girls seem to be higher in goal orientation or the desire to achieve personal goals while boys seem to be more motivated by winning. Many girls prefer activities that allow them to work together to improve, or to function cooperatively to accomplish goals (Jaffee &Manzer, 1992), rather than competitive activities such as physical fitness testing (Wiese-Bjornstal, 1997). It is therefore important to structure daily physical activity experiences to provide motivation for children who have both goal and win orientations.

During adolescence there appears to emerge a gender difference such that girls rely on adults and their own self-comparisons, while boys seem to rely more on competitive outcomes, their ability to learn new skills and their own ego-centric judgments of physical competence (Weiss &Ebbeck, 1996). These differences suggest the important role of parents, teachers and coaches in influencing girls attitudes toward participation.

Participation in sport and physical activity has a positive effect on emotional wellbeing. Children who are depressed or having emotional problems benefit from increased levels of physical activity (Biddle, 1995), with benefits reported to lower levels of depression (Morgan, 1994) and general anxiety (Landers &Petruzzello, 1994). The effects of participation in an active life style may have both a beneficial treatment effect, and also a palliative or buffering effect prior to any onset of emotional problems (Wiese-Bjornstal, examining the research literature regarding the influence of physical activity on depression and anxiety (Singer, 1992). Physical activity can help reduce anxiety, help decrease mild to moderate depression, help reduce anxiety, reduce various types of stress, and have beneficial emotional effects. In addition, regular physical activity and its body composition benefits may also result in increased energy and improved sleep patterns (Martinsen &Stephens, 1994) and a general feeling of self- accomplishment for sticking to goals and developing new skills (Koniak-Griffin. Sport and physical activity can provide a great venue for exploring strategies to resolve conflicts, act fairly, plan proactively, and to generally develop a moral code of behavior. Opportunities exist for children to experience their own decision-making and to observe other role models such as parents, coaches and other athletes and to get feedback about their own ethical behaviors (Martens, 1993). There are many opportunities for good moral development through sport and physical activity, especially when these opportunities are provided under adult guidance and structured to support positive growth and avoid the potential negative impact of anti-social behaviors (cheating, aggression and intimidation) that accompany some inappropriately competitive activities (Gibbons, Ebbeck &Weiss, 1995). Sport can be a great avenue for developing more mature moral reasoning skills that are characterized by more assertion and less aggression, and more compliance with rules and fair play (Stephens & Bredemeier, 1996). Some children love low levels of competition while others are psychologically ready for higher levels of competition when they want to compare their skills with others and when they can understand the competitive process (Passer, 1988).

The U.S. Department of Health and Human Services has several ongoing initiatives and programs to address women's health issues throughout its agencies, including the National Institutes of Health (NIH), the Centers for Disease Control and Prevention (CDC), and the Office of Women's Health (OWH) within the Office of the Assistant Secretary for Health. These agencies participate in the Women's Health Coordinating Committee as do the women's health components of many other HHS agencies. I want to share with you today a few notable HHS initiatives that concern physical activity and health for women and girls.

The results of the Health and Growth Study, funded by the National Heart, Lung, and Blood Institute of the NIH, showed that a decline in physical activity plays key role in weight gain among adolescent girls. Girls who were inactive during adolescence gained an average of 10 to 15 pounds more than active girls, according to results of the 10-year observational study of obesity. Total calorie intake increased only slightly and was not associated with the weight gains. These results show that a previously reported steep decline in physical activity among adolescent girls is directly associated with increased fatness and an increase of body mass index (BMI), a measure of body weight adjusted for height. The NHLBI has launched "We Can! — Ways to Enhance Children's Activity and Nutrition" — a childhood obesity prevention program designed to encourage parents and children to adopt healthy eating habits, increase physical activity, and reduce leisure "screen time". More than 35 communities across the country are integrating "We Can!" lessons into health programming for parents and kids.

The CDC, the HHS Office Women's Health, and the National Osteoporosis Foundation (NOF) have partnered on an initiative, the National Bone Health Campaign ("Powerful Bones. Powerful Girls" ^{TM}) . This program uses a social marketing approach to promote optimal bone health among girls 9–12 years of age in an effort to reduce their risk of osteoporosis later in life. The campaign's purpose is to encourage girls to establish lifelong healthy habits, focusing on increased calcium consumption and weight-bearing physical activity to build and maintain strong bones. Parents and other adults close to girls play an important role by encouraging girls to take action. Resources for this campaign include a Web site for girls, and print materials, radio and print advertisements for girls and parents.

The HHS Office on Women's Health has also developed the GirlsHealth.gov web site, which promotes healthy, positive behaviors in girls between the ages of 10 and 16. The site gives girls reliable, useful information on the health issues they will face as they become young women, including physical activity and sports. The site offers tips on handling relationships with family and friends, at school and at home. It focuses on health topics that girls are concerned about and helps motivate them to choose healthy behaviors by using positive, supportive, and non-threatening messages.

Finally, I want to tell you about the President's Challenge, the motivational awards program of the President's Council on Physical Fitness and Sports. As the Council members and I travel around the country, we want to do more than quote health statistics. We are offering a *tool* to get all Americans, including women and girls, to start moving *today*. That tool is the "President's Challenge," a program to motivate everyone to start moving today and stay active for a lifetime.

You, Senators, and your colleagues, staff, family and friends can participate in the Challenge by logging on to presidentschallenge.org and signing up to earn a Presidential Active Lifestyle Award (PALA) for activity on five or more days a week for six weeks (30 minutes for adults, 60 minutes a day for youth aged 6- 17). For those who are already active, the Presidential Champions awards offer bronze, silver and gold medals for points earned through participating in one or more of over 100 activities.

Every activity counts toward the awards— walking, climbing the stairs, raking leaves, digging in the garden, mopping the floor, biking, playing tag, dancing, jumping rope, sports-- any physical activity! And you don't have to do it at one time — you can accumulate activities in smaller increments. Take the President's Challenge yourself and challenge your family to join you; challenge your constituents and staff to join you. Particularly, I call on you today to challenge the women in your life to start moving for health and well-being today--at home, at school, at work, at play and leisure, and in retirement communities and senior centers.

Please, tell your constituents to "Be physically active every day." Tell them in your speeches and press conferences -- any time you speak about health. Please promote the active lifestyle, promote a *HealthierUS*. Together, step-by-step, day-by-day, we can build a healthier U.S. for Americans of all ages, backgrounds and abilities, men and women, boys and girls alike.

Thank you for the opportunity to testify this morning. I would be happy to respond to questions.

REFERENCES AND RESOURCES

[1]   Armstrong, N., & Weissman, J. R. (1994). Assessment and interpretation of aerobic fitness in children and adolescents. In J.E. Holloszy (Ed.), Exercise and Sport Science Review. (pp. 435-476). *Philadelphia: Williams and Wilkins.*

[2]   Bar-Or, O., & Malina, R. M. (1995). Activity, fitness, and health of

children and adolescents. In L.W. Y. *Cheung & J.B. Richmond (Eds),*
Child health, nutrition, and physical activity. (pp. 79-1 23). Champaign,
IL: Human Kinetics Publishers.

[3]   Berryman, J. (1996). The rise of boys' sports in the United states, 1900-
1970. In F. Smoll & R. Smith (Eds). *Children and Youth in Sports: A*
Biopsychosocial Perspective. Dubuque, IA: Brown and Benchmarks.

[4]   Biddle, S. (1995). Exercise and psychosocial health. *Research Quarterly*
for Exercise and Sport, 66(4), 292-297.

[5]   Blair, S. N., Horton, E., Leon, A. S., Lee, I.-M., Drinkwater, B.
L.,Dishman, R. D., Mackey, M., & Keinholz, M.L. (1996). Physical ac-
tivity, nutrition and chronic disease. *Medicine and Science in Sports and*
Exercise, 28, 335- 349.

[6]   Blimkie, C. J. R. (1989). Age and sex associated variation in strength
during childhood: Anthropometric, morphologic, neurologic, biomechanical, endcrinologic, and physical activity correlates. In C.V. Gisolfi
& D. R. Lamb (Eds), *Perspectives in exercise science and sports medi-*
cine volume 2: Youth exercise and sport (pp 99-1 63). Indianapolis:
Benchmark.

[7]   Brustad, R. J. (1993). Youth in sports: Psychological considerations. In
R.N. Singer, Murphey & L. K. tenneant (Eds.*) Handbook of research on*
sorts psychology. (695-71 7). New York: Macmillan Publishing Co.

[8]   Fehily, A. M., Coles, R. J., Evans, W. D., Elwood, P. C. (1992) *Factors*
affecting bone density in young adults. American Journal of Clinical Nutrition, 56, 579-586.

[9]   Freedson, P. & Bunker, L.K. (1997). *Section I: Physiological dimen-*
sions. In the President's Council on Physical Fitness and Sport, Physical
Activity and Sport in the Lives of Girls. (pp 1-16). Washington, DC:
President's Council.

[10]   Garcia, C. (1994). Gender differences in young children's interactions
when learning fundamental motor skills. *Research Quarterly for Exer-*
cise and Sport, 65(3), 225.

[11]   Gibbons, S. L., Ebbeck, V., & Weiss, M.R. (1995). Fair play for kids:
Effects on the moral development of children in physical education. *Re-*
search Quarterly for Exercise and Sport, 66(3), 247-255.

[12]   Gill, D. L. (1992). Gender and sport behavior. In T. S. Horn (Ed.), *Ad-*
vances in sport psychology (pp. 143-1 60). Champaign, IL: Human Kinetics Publishers.

[13]   Gill, D. L. (1995). Gender issues: A social-educational perspective. In
S.M. Murphy (Ed.), *Sport psychology interventions* (pp. 205-234).

Champaign, IL: Human Kinetics Publishers.

[14] Gould, D. (1993). Intensive sport participation and the prepubescent athlete: Competitive stress and burnout. In B.R. Cahill & A.J. Pearl (Eds.), *Intensive participation in children's sports* (pp.19-38). Champaign, IL: Human Kinetics Publishers.

[15] Greenberg, D. & Oglesby, C. (1997). Section IV: Mental health dimensions. In the President's Council on *Physical Fitness and Sport, Physical Activity and Sport in the Lives of Girls.* (pp 1-16). Washington, DC: President's Council.

[16] Greist, J. H., & Jefferson, J. W. (1992). *Depression and Its Treatment* (Rev. Ed.). Washington, DC: American Psychiatric Press.

[17] Jaffee, L., & Manzer, R. (1992). Girls' perspectives: Physical activity and self-esteem. Melpomene: A Journal for Women's Health Research, *11*(3), 14-23.

[18] Jaffee, L., & Wu, P. (1996). After school activities and self-esteem in adolescent girls. Melpomene: *A Journal for Women's Health Research, 15*(2), 18-25.

[19] Koniak-Griffin, D. (1994). Aerobic exercise, psychological well-being, and physical discomforts during adolescent pregnancy. *Research in Nursing & Health, 17,* 253-263.

[20] Kramer, M. M. & Wells, C. L. (1996). Does physical activity reduce risk of estrogendependent cancer in women? *Medicine and Science in Sports and Exercise, 28,* 322-334.

[21] Landers, D. M., & Petruzzello, S. J. (1994). Physical activity, fitness and anxiety. In C. Bouchard, R.J. Shepard, &

[22] T. Stephens (Eds.), *Physical activity fitness and health* (pp. 868-882). Champaign, IL: Human Kinetics Publishers.

[23] Martens, R. (1993). Psychological perspectives. In B.R. Cahill & A.J. Pearl (Eds.), *Intensive participation in children's sports* (pp. 9-17). Champaign, IL: Human Kinetics Publishers.

[24] Martinsen, E. W., & Stephens, T. (1994). Exercise and mental health in clinical and free-living populations. In R.K. Dishman (Ed.), *Advances in exercise adherence* (pp. 55-72). Champaign, IL: Human Kinetics Publishers.

[25] Morgan, W. P. (1994). Physical activity, fitness and depression. In C. Bouchard, R.J. Shepard, & T. Stephens (Eds.), *Physical activity, fitness and health* (pp. 851 -867). Champaign, IL: Human Kinetics Publishers.

[26] National Cholesterol Education Program. (1991). *Report of the expert panel on blood cholesterol levels in children and adolescents.* (NIH Pub-

lication No. 91-2732). Bethesda, MD: National, Heart, Lung and Blood Institute.

[27] National Federation of State High Schools Association. (1995-96). *The National Federation of State High School Associations Handbook*, 1995-96. Kansas City, MO: NFSHSA.

[28] Newsholme, E. A., & Parry-Billings, M. (1994). Effects of exercise on the immune system. In C. Bouchard, R. J. Shephard, & T. Stephens (Eds). Physical activity, fitness and health: International proceedings and consensus statement (pp 451-455). Champaign, IL: Human Kinetics Publishers Nieman, D.C. (1994). Exercise, upper respiratory infection, and the immune system. *Medicine and Science in Sports and Exercise, 26,* 1057-1 062.

[29] North, T. C., McCullaugh, P., & Tran, Z. U. (1990). Effects of exercise on depression. *Exercise and Sport Science Reviews, 18,* 379-415.

[30] Oler, M. J., Mainous III, A. G., Martin, C. A., Richardson, E., Haney, A., Wilson, D., & Adams, T. (1994). Depression, suicidal ideation, and substance use among adolescents: Are adolescents at less risk? *Archives of Family Medicine, 3,* 781-785.

[31] Passer, M. W. (1988). Psychological issues in determining children's age- readiness for competition. In F.L. Smoll, R.A. Magill, & M.J. Ash (Eds). *Children in sports* (pp 203-227).

[32] Plaisted, V. (1995). Gender and sport. In T. Morris & J. Summers (Eds.), *Sport psychology: theory, applications and* issues (pp. 538-574). New York: John Wiley & Sons.

[33] President's Council on Physical Fitness and Sports (1997a). *Physical Activity and Sport in the Lives of Girls: Physical and Mental Health dimensions from an Interdisciplinary Approach.* Washington, DC: Department of Health and Human Services.

[34] President's Council on Physical Fitness and Sports (1997b). *Executive Summary of Physical Activity and Sport in the Lives of Girls: Physical and Mental Health dimensions from an Interdisciplinary Approach.* Washington, DC: Department of Health and Human Services.

[35] Reel, J. J. & Gill, D. L. (1996). Psychosocial factors related to eating disorders among high school and college female cheerleaders. *The Sport Psychologist, 10,* 195-206.

[36] Sale, D. G. (1989). Strength training in children. In C.V. Gisolfi & D. R. Lam (Eds.), *Perspectives in exercise science and sports medicine. Vol 2:* Youth, exercise, and sport (pp. 165-222). Indianapolis, Benchmark Press.

[37] Sewall, L., & Micheli, L. J. (1986). Strength training for children. *The Journal of Pediatric Orthopaedia Strabismus, 6,* 143-146.

[38] Shepard, R.J. (1984). Physical activity and child health. *Sports Medicine, 1,* 205-233.

[39] Singer, R. S. (1992). Physical activity and psychological benefits: A position statement of the International Society of Sport Psychology (ISSP). *The Sports Psychologist, 6,* 199-203.

[40] Stager, J. M., Wigglesworth, J. K., & Hatler, L. H. (1990). Interpreting the relationship between age of menarche and prepubertal training. *Medicine and Science in Sports and Exercise, 22,* 54-58.

[41] Stephens, D., & Bredemeier, B. J. (1996). Moral atmosphere and judgments about aggression in girls' soccer: Relationships among moral and motivational variables. *Journal of Sport and Exercise Physiology, 18*(2), 158-171.

[42] Thorne, B. (1993). *Gender play: Girls and boys in school.* New Brunswick, NJ: Rutgers University Press.

[43] Weiss, M. R., & Ebbeck, V. (1996). Self-esteem and perceptions of competence in youth sports: Theory, research and enhancement strategies. In O.Bar-Or (Ed.), *The child and adolescent athlete* (pp. 364- 382). Oxford, England: Blackwell Scientific Ltd.

[44] Weiss, M. R., & Petlichkoff, L. M. (1989). Children's motivation for participation in and withdrawal from sport: Identifying the missing links. *Pediatric Exercise Science, 1,* 195-211.

[45] Wells, C.L. (1991). *Women, sport and performance,* 2 ed. Champaign, IL: Human Kinetics Publishers.

[46] Wiese-Bjornstal, D. (1997). Section II: Psychological dimensions. In the President's Council on *Physical fitness and Sport report Physical Activity and Sport in the Lives of Girls.* (pp. 49-69). Washington, D.C.: President's Council.

[47] Williams, D. P., Going, S. B., Lohman, T. G., Harsha, D. W., Srinivasan, S. R., Webber, L. S., & Berenson, G. S. (1992). Body fatness and risk for elevated blood pressure total cholesterol and serum lipoprotein ratios in children and adolescents. *American Journal of Public Health, 82,* 358-363.

[48] Women's Sports Foundation Report: Minorities in sports. (1989). East Meadow, NY: Women's Sports Foundation.

In: Women in Sports pp. 165-170
Editors: Amelia S. Halloway

ISBN: 978-1-61728-161-7
© 2010 Nova Science Publishers, Inc.

Chapter 16

STATEMENT OF JUDITH M. SWEET, SENIOR VICE-PRESIDENT FOR CHAMPIONSHIPS AND EDUCATION SERVICES, NATIONAL COLLEGIATE ATHLETIC ASSOCIATION, BEFORE THE COMMITTEE ON COMMERCE, SCIENCE AND TRANSPORTATION ON PROMOTION AND ADVANCEMENT OF WOMEN IN SPORTS

Judith M. Sweet

Chairman Stevens, Ranking Member Inouye and other distinguished members of the Committee, on behalf of the National Collegiate Athletic Association (NCAA), thank you for inviting me to appear before you today to discuss the advancement of women in athletics.

I am Judith Sweet, and I currently serve as NCAA Senior Vice President for Championships and Education Services. I have been involved in intercollegiate athletics and higher education for more than 30 years as an athletic administrator, academician and in leadership roles within the NCAA. During my tenure in the field of intercollegiate athletics, I have worked extensively on matters involving the growth of opportunities and advancement of both men and women in athletics. The gap in opportunities and support remains greater for women and thus more needs to be done to ensure parity. Through my work, I have seen first-hand the commitment of the NCAA and many universities to promote equity and consequently the resulting strides which have been made in the pursuit of gender equity on campuses and NCAA programs. I am pleased with the progress, excited about the future, but wary of efforts to undo more than three decades of work.

THAT WAS THEN

Thirty-four years ago, when Title IX first became law, there were no NCAA championships for women. There were no college athletics scholarships to speak of for women and there were few opportunities for competition. There was virtually no media coverage of the few competitive opportunities that did exist and certainly no television coverage. It was rare for newsstand publications to carry any type of article about a female athlete, and there were no publications devoted to women's sports. The star athletes in college sports were often household names, but none of them was a woman. The female athlete as a role model was virtually unheard of. A young boy wouldn't be caught dead wearing a jersey with a woman's name on the back, even if they had existed.

The athletics opportunities for women were few; and the prospects for growth were dismal. According to a 1971-72 survey of NCAA member institutions, only 29,977 women were participating in sports and recreation programs, compared to 170,384 men – more than five times as many men as women. With numbers like that, it would be fair to wonder why college women would show any interest at all in athletics.

THIS IS NOW

What a difference 34 years and legislative impetus make. Throughout 2006 the NCAA is celebrating its centennial and the 25th anniversary of NCAA women's championships. Today, nearly 160,000 women are competing in sports at NCAA member institutions. As new opportunities for girls and women have been made available at the high school and college levels, participation has escalated. The NCAA offers 88 championships in 23 sports for men and women. Forty-four of those championships in 20 sports are exclusively for women and there are three co-educational championships. Growing interest has sparked the creation of additional NCAA championships since the 26 it first offered in 1981. The NCAA added women's rowing to the championships ranks in 1996, followed by women's ice hockey and women's water polo in 2001 and women's bowling in 2003.

In 1982 the Women's Final Four drew 9,531 fans. In 2005, the Women's Final Four at the RCA Dome in Indianapolis drew a sellout crowd of 28,937 – just a thousand less than the total number of women participating in college sports 34 years earlier. It was the third time the Women's Final Four had appeared in a dome, but it was the 15th consecutive sellout in Women's Final Four history. Almost 700 media credentials were issued, and television covered the event from selection Sunday through the final buzzer.

According to a recent membership survey, women now account for 43 percent of the participants in intercollegiate athletics and receive about 45 percent of the scholarship dollars.

Female athletes such as Dominique Dawes, Jennie Finch, Cat Reddick and Julie Foudy have, in fact, become household names in their own right. Elite female athletes play professional basketball in the WNBA. The women's teams from the United States are expected to bring home a sizeable haul of medals in most sports in every Olympics, and young girls – and boys – proudly wore Mia Hamm's No. 9 at the 1999 Women's World Cup and during the last two Olympics.

While mainstream media still devotes much more attention to men's sports, the average bookstore now includes magazines and books highlighting the accomplishments of women in sports. Most of the student-athletes – female or male – competing in NCAA championships probably don't think twice about the NCAA offering championships for women and are unaware of how opportunities for women have changed over the last three decades.

Clearly, Title IX has promoted opportunities for female athletes over the last 30 years.

MORE WORK REMAINS

In its charge to the Commission on Opportunity in Athletics in 2001, the Department of Education acknowledged that extraordinary progress has resulted from the passage of Title IX. While I would like to think that this change would have taken place without Title IX because it was the right thing to do, the fact is that opportunities and support for girls and women in athletics are still not equitable with those provided for men, even though it is more than 30 years since the law was passed.

The results of federal law and the hard work of campus leaders have been impressive over the last 34 years, but there is much work still to be done to ensure that men and women who attend NCAA member schools have equitable access to athletics participation and receive related support. Although women comprise 54 percent of the undergraduate student population at NCAA member schools on average, they represent only 43 percent of the participating student-athletes, receive only 38 percent of the operating dollars and have only 33 percent of the recruiting budgets.

The bottom line is: Women are still the underrepresented gender in college sports and less funding is devoted to the support of women's programs.

In the years since it began sponsoring NCAA championships, the NCAA has taken a progressively more active role in assisting its members with gender-equity matters. In 1992, after publication of the first NCAA Gender-Equity Study, the NCAA executive director established a gender-equity task force and charged it with determining ways in which the NCAA could assist institutions in achieving gender equity, examining NCAA policies to evaluate their impact on gender equity and recommending a path toward measuring and realizing gender equity in intercollegiate athletics. One of the recommendations of the task force was the creation of a sourcebook for NCAA members. That sourcebook, "Achieving Gender Equity: A Basic Guide to Title IX and Gender Equity in Athletics for Colleges and Universities," is now in its third edition. It is free to NCAA members and includes information on current case law, the basics of Title IX compliance, information about NCAA emerging sports and even promotional ideas for women's sports.

This spring, the NCAA will conduct its 15th Title IX Seminar/Gender Equity Issues Forum since 1995. These now annual seminars are designed to assist NCAA member schools in understanding the intent of Title IX and to provide them with the necessary educational resources needed so they can comply with the law and address other gender equity issues. The Association has placed emphasis on institutional gender-equity plans through the Division I certification process and the Divisions II and III self-study processes. And, in 1994, legislation was passed that identified "emerging sports" for women that, while not yet sponsored by member schools in sufficient numbers to create a championship, counted in other important ways for institutions in terms of revenue distribution and sports-sponsorship numbers. The intent was to further increase the menu of sports available for women and encourage institutions to increase opportunities for women by sponsoring these sports, several of which have recently become NCAA championships as a result. Once again, as opportunities have been made available, participation by women has increased significantly.

At the same time, the NCAA has increased the minimum number of sports sponsored for both men and women as part of an institution's Division I membership requirements. The Association's revenue-distribution plan recognizes the value of broad-based programs, both in terms of the number of sports and the number of athletics grants-in-aid. In 1996, the NCAA membership established a moratorium that precluded the discontinuation of any championships through 1998-99, thus protecting both men's and women's Olympic sports where sponsorship had declined. The moratorium was replaced in 1997 by legislation that specifies that even if sponsorship for an Olympic sport drops below minimum established requirements (40 schools for championships established before 1995 and 50 for those thereafter), the championship remains unless the membership specifically votes to dissolve it. This action shows strong support on the part of NCAA members to maintain Olympic sports as part of the NCAA championships program even though individual members may have chosen to no longer sponsor an Olympic sport.

CONCLUSION

In a perfect world, Title IX would not be necessary. There would be resources and will enough to do the right thing and meet everyone's needs. Social legislation exists, of course, because we do not live in that perfect world. Even with more than 30 years of experience and the examples of the several hundred thousand female student-athletes who have benefited from increased athletics participation for women, threats to the future of Title IX remain.

The most recent and one of the most pernicious examples is the so-called "additional clarification" letter of 2005 issued by the Department of Education without prior announcement or opportunity for public comment on the additional clarification. The Department of Education now allows institutions of higher education to rely solely on an Internet-based survey to measure interest in athletics among their students. Notoriously unreliable as valid instruments for measurement, these e-mail surveys would interpret a non-response the same as a "no" response that is, as an indication that there is no interest in additional sports opportunities. This approach is contrary to the intent of Title IX itself and appears to be designed to enable schools to show that females are not interested in participation as opposed to the previous 1996 clarification which allowed for surveys but only as one of multiple components as an assessment of interest. The effect of this recent survey approach potentially would be to freeze participation opportunities at their current level or worse to roll back the progress made over the last 34 years. NCAA President Myles Brand and the NCAA Executive Committee, the highest decision making body of the association comprised of university presidents from throughout the country, have notified the Department of Education of their deep concerns about the flaws in the additional clarification and have asked that it be withdrawn. The Department of Education reaffirmed the 1996 clarification in 2003 and should not be allowed to lessen that commitment now.

The standard for measuring success for 2006 and beyond is the same as that set by a NCAA Gender-Equity Task Force in 1992. It defined gender equity in the following manner: "An athletics program can be considered gender equitable when the participants in both the men's and women's programs would accept as fair and equitable the overall program of the other gender."

I am proud of how far we have come. Thanks to the efforts of people like Christine Grant, Donna deVarona and Dot Richardson, female student-athletes can hope for the same educational experience that males have enjoyed and benefited from for generations. Title IX is a real success story. But as successful as this important federal legislation has been, those who value fair, equitable treatment must remain vigilant to any and all threats that would undermine future progress.

Thank you for the opportunity to appear before you today.

CHAPTER SOURCES

The following chapters have been previously published:

Chapter 4 – This is an edited, reformatted and augmented edition of testimony made before the U.S. Senate Committee on Commerce, Science and Transportation on Promotion and Advancement of Women in Sports by Marcia D. Greenberger on June 19, 2007.

Chapter 5 – This is an edited, reformatted and augmented edition of testimony made before the U.S. Senate Committee on Commerce, Science and Transportation on Promotion and Advancement of Women in Sports by Jack Mowatt on June 19, 2007.

Chapter 6 – This is an edited, reformatted and augmented edition of a National Institutes of Health, Osteoporosis and Related Bone Diseases, National Resources Center publication of May 2009.

Chapter 7 – This is an edited, reformatted and augmented edition of a Congressional Research Service publication, CRS Report RL31709, dated January 12, 2010.

Chapter 8 – This is an edited, reformatted and augmented edition of statements made before the U.S. Senate Committee on Commerce, Science and Transportation on Promotion and Advancement of Women in Sports by Dominique Dawes on February 1, 2006.

Chapter 9 – This is an edited, reformatted and augmented edition of statements made before the U.S. Senate Committee on Commerce, Science and Transportation on Promotion and Advancement of Women in Sports by Donna de Varona on February 1, 2006.

Chapter 10 – This is an edited, reformatted and augmented edition of testimony made before the U.S. Senate Committee on Commerce, Science and

Transportation on Promotion and Advancement of Women in Sports by Tara Erickson on February 1, 2006.

Chapter 11 – This is an edited, reformatted and augmented edition of statements made before the U.S. Senate Committee on Commerce, Science and Transportation on Promotion and Advancement of Women in Sports by Jennie Finch on February 1, 2006.

Chapter 12 – This is an edited, reformatted and augmented edition of statements made before the U.S. Senate Committee on Commerce, Science and Transportation on Promotion and Advancement of Women in Sports by Christine Grant on February 1, 2006.

Chapter 13 – This is an edited, reformatted and augmented edition of testimony made before the U.S. Senate Committee on Commerce, Science and Transportation on Promotion and Advancement of Women in Sports by Lynette Mund on February 1, 2006.

Chapter 14 – This is an edited, reformatted and augmented edition of testimony made before the U.S. Senate Committee on Commerce, Science and Transportation on Promotion and Advancement of Women in Sports by Catherine Anne Reddick on February 1, 2006.

Chapter 15 – This is an edited, reformatted and augmented edition of testimony made before the U.S. Senate Committee on Commerce, Science and Transportation on Promotion and Advancement of Women in Sports by Dorothy G. Richardson on February 1, 2006.

Chapter 16 – This is an edited, reformatted and augmented edition of statements made before the U.S. Senate Committee on Commerce, Science and Transportation on Promotion and Advancement of Women in Sports by Judith M. Sweet on February 1, 2006.

INDEX